Islam and Gender Politics in Iran

Islam and Gender Politics in Iran

By

Jyotika Teckchandani
Assistant Professor,
Amity Institute of Social Sciences,
Amity University, Noida

New Century Publications
New Delhi, India

New Century Publications
4800/24, Bharat Ram Road,
Ansari Road, Daryaganj,
New Delhi - 110 002 (India)

Tel.: 011-2324 7798, 4358 7398
Fax: 011-4101 7798
E-mail: indiatax@vsnl.com • info@newcenturypublications.com
www.newcenturypublications.com

Editorial office:
LG–7, Aakarshan Bhawan,
4754-57/23, Ansari Road, Daryaganj,
New Delhi – 110 002

Tel.: 011-4356 0919

First Published: **2017**

ISBN: **978-81-7708-438-2**

Published by New Century Publications and printed at Salasar Imaging Systems, New Delhi.

Designs: Patch Creative Unit, New Delhi.

PRINTED IN INDIA

About the Book

This study explores the linkages between religion, gender and nation and examines them in the context of the Islamic Republic of Iran (IRI). Contrary to popular perception, it treats that state, gender and religion—particularly Islam—are not monolithic categories and demonstrates that the relationship among them is one of dynamic interactive processes without any fixed pattern. It brings out the implications of interplay of gender, religion, class, and ideologies for negotiating the privileges and rights of women within the existing polity and power structure of Iran.

Contrary to dominant Western narrative about the perpetual marginalization of women in Iran, the present work claims that contraction or expansion of women's rights and privileges depend upon the nature of political regime, strength of women's movements and socio-economic dynamics of the Iranian society.

About the Author

Dr. Jyotika Teckchandani is currently an Assistant Professor at Amity Institute of Social Sciences, Amity University, Noida. She did her B.A. (Hons.) in Political Science from Sri Venkateswara College, and M.A. in Political Science from Lady Shri Ram College, both affiliated to University of Delhi. She received her M.Phil. and Ph.D. degrees on West Asian Studies from Jamia Millia Islamia, New Delhi. She has contributed a number of articles in academic journals of repute and newspapers including *Indian Journal of Secularism, Journal of West Asian Studies* and *Pioneer.* Her research interests include gender studies, West Asian politics, and political theory and thought.

Contents

Preface

Gender Studies is an important emerging discipline in the field of contemporary social science. Under the spell of post-modernism there is an increasing focus to understand gender mediated social realities and highlight the intersection between gender, identity, class, religion and its method of negotiation with power structure. This study intends to be a small contribution in this direction. The Islamic revolution of Iran primarily drew the attention of western scholars from the point of view of its negative impact on women's freedom that was supposedly gained during the Shah's period. Most of such studies highlight the marginalized and subordinate position of women or women's victimhood in Iranian society under Islamic Republic.

Not many studies have been conducted on how gender is utilized for nation-building process and how through 'gendering politics' women negotiate with the existing power structure that sometimes results in contraction of their rights and privileges and sometimes expands the same. This study intends to demonstrate the complex process of gendering politics in Iranian society that includes the interplay of gender-identity, religion, class, ideologies and political participation that has implication for negotiating with the existing polity and power structure and emerging nation-building process in post Khomeini Iran. Since 1989, the Iranian polity has undergone qualitative political, economic and social changes that have impacted the gender discourses and relationship in Iranian society. The work attempts to analyze the ways in which these changes have affected the role, position and condition of women in Islamic Republic of Iran (IRI) in post-Khomeini period. In addition, the study also reflects upon the nature of women's movements in Iran in post-Khomeini period.

Women Studies and Gender Studies: A Clarification: A review of the available literature provides an insight on how gender issues are important in Iran and are therefore helpful for the present study. However, they are deficient in terms of understanding of 'gendering politics' involving both state and non state actors. None of these literatures provides a detailed understanding and analysis of how gender is used in political conflicts, legitimization, nation-building and competition over state power. There are two principal shortcomings that most of the studies, some of which has been examined above, on gender-state relations in Islamic Republic of Iran suffer. A bulk of these studies has tried to examine the gender-state relationship within the framework of 'women studies' that entails an account of either marginalized or enhanced position of women in various fields of life- social, political and economic- in comparison to the Shah's period in Iran.

This work has proceeded on the sharp distinction between gender studies and women studies that have surfaced in the recent years. Women studies focus on the empowerment of women in terms of socio economic and political indicators without changing the dominant patriarchal values that shapes the state actions. Women studies are about sharing in the national resources and power structure of the country whereas gender studies are about transforming the values. In gender studies, the focus is to construct a gender friendly or gender inclusive nation building process and nation state. In gender studies the condition and status of women are examined from inter-gender perspective. In this sense, gender study is primarily about democratizing the social and political process with a view to ensure a more meaningful participation of women in formal as well as informal spaces.

Within this broader perspective the term 'gender politics' has two specific interlinked connotations: 'politics of gender' and 'genderization of politics'. The former refers to the political use of gender by the state actors for constructing a particular nation or national identity. Thus, relative liberal and conservative state's policies on women partly flow partly from politics of imagined nation. The latter is an attempt on the part of women movements and actors to make the nation-building process much more inclusive and to make the state more gender friendly or gender neutral in order to take into consideration the various concerns of women. The 'politics of gender' and 'genderization of politics' are interlinked as they interact and impact each other.

Islam, State and Gender: Not a Monolithic Entity: A second shortcoming in gender-state relationship in Iran is that a majority of literatures, some of which has been examined above, has treated state agency, gender and Islam as fixed entity and has then proceeded to examine the impact of state policies on women in the uniform manner in terms of top-bottom structure. However neither state, Islam nor gender is a monolithic entity; rather they are heterogeneous in terms of interest, factions, class and imaginations. Further all these three categories are fluid and thus interacts and impacts each other. Certainly state/government is an organization involved in the exercise of political domination and hegemony including its monopoly over coercive apparatus of the political and social system and embodies its own interests, ideology and structures. However, being relatively autonomous these components may undergo changes because the state being a fluid, it responds to its environment in different ways. The state is not a single-minded actor with a unified set of interests. States are composed of different, conflicting, and changing sets of interests and without any fixed relationship with gender.

State, Gender and Nation-Building: The linkage between gender and nation is mediated through the administrative agency of state. As the identity of nation is far from settled in most of societies, particularly in post-colonial societies, it is the state that fashions and refashions the construction of nation-building in the society. It is in the process of politics of 'imagined' nation-building that various governments differentially impact the gender relationship in the society depending upon its ideological world-view, social base and nature of factional politics. Thus state or government uses women and their portrayal to ensure the multiple purposes: depict a distinct political identity of the 'imagined' nation such as secular or religious, traditional or modern or westernized and Islamized, to legitimize its cultural and political position/values and to consolidate its power and deals with political opponents.

Women's position and status, to a large extent, depends on their relationship with the state and their responses to state policies. In other words, how and where women figures in the overall power structure of state determines the condition and status of women in the society. This is more particular in the context of developing societies like Iran where state assumes the role of social transformation of society. Depending upon the ideological propensities and material social base, the state unleashes the programme for expanding or contracting gender specific opportunity structure. In the process, the state sets an agenda for the control of particular class of women or their activities. It builds alliances with different classes of women especially in their policies of mobilization. Thus, the Islamic Republic mobilized the poor, traditional (Bazaari) and the working class women and ignored the interests of the urban educated middle class women.

Although the state has the ability to modify and reshape gender relations and women's lives, its actions however, are limited by the persistence of women's resistance. As active and reactive agents of social change, women respond to and defy state actions. Women pose challenges to the system, constraining and modifying the state's behaviour—sometimes successfully, sometimes not. Women's responses vary historically, not only by their class background, ideological dispositions, and religious outlook, but by the degree of their political and feminist awareness and also how they can articulate their interests and issues of their concerns. Thus, gender can be seen through a state lens both in its domestic and international environments, and conversely, the state can be analyzed through its gender policies and women's experiences.

Gender Politics in Islamic Republic of Iran: Principle of Expansion and Contraction of Women Rights: The discourse on gender relations in post-revolutionary Iran is very complex and cuts the dominant binary framework of tradition vs. modernity. The Islamic Republic did not inherit a readymade Islamic policy on Gender. The dominant conceptions of gender were constructed as events developed in post-revolutionary society. Gender relations in IRI can be described as volatile and contentious. There is no singular explanation of "Islamic gender ideology". Throughout Islamic history, author's interpretations of 'women in Islam' have been influenced as much by *Qur'anic* axioms and *Hadith* narratives as by authors own socio-historical specificities. [1] In 1963, Ayatollah Khomeini reacted vehemently to women's enfranchisement. But in 1979, Ayatollah finally recognized women's political role and solicited their vote for establishing an Islamic Government. Thus, in both the cases his ideas were based on Islamic principles, different times and contexts however made conflicting interpretations possible.

The road from 1979 has been a very challenging one for the Iranian women. Compulsory veiling, ban on women singers, exclusion from political power, economic marginalization and the return of unilateral divorce, promotion of polygamy and temporary marriage were some of the major gender policies that characterized the first ten years of the Islamic Revolution. IRI initially attempted to shift the gender relations in Iran back to private patriarchy and sought to reinforce male dominance within the family, reinstate men's prerogative and define women primarily in their private roles of a wife and a mother. However, women's social role in the pre revolutionary Iran has made it impossible to send them back to the home. Though successful in passing legislations that limited women's options, Islamists were forced to accept results of the 1986 national census of population and housing showed clearly a decline in female labour force participation, particularly in the industrial sector, soaring fertility increases and population growth, a sex ratio that favoured males. Male domination in the family was strengthened by Islamisation, and women's familial rights diminished leading to a significant deterioration of the living conditions of women.

Moreover, Islamic notion of Muslim womanhood and Islamic moral values failed to win over the woman. Many women supporters of the regime also realized that the idealized notion of an Islamic way of life had helped to create a political order that legally undermined women in marriage, family and the work place. Many Islamist women (commonly known as Islamic feminists) also became the advocates of women's rights. The policies of the regime created a gender awareness and resistance on the part of its female citizens.

With the end of war with Iraq in 1988 and particularly after the death of Ayatollah Khomeini, policies of IRI underwent significant change. The growing women protest and deteriorating economic conditions due to a long war with Iraq and other hardships of human life forced the government to rethink and reverse its initial exclusionist-protectivist orientation towards women. There was also an increase in the demand for female labour in education and health along with the divisions within the political elite.

The changes began after the death of Ayatollah Khomeini and continued during the presidency of Hashemi Rafsanjani (1989-1997), in the context of economic liberalization and integration into the global economy. During this time, Iranian civil society had developed and a lively women's press emerged. Many barriers to women's educational achievement and their employment were removed. In education, the IRI had to revise its initial banning of numerous majors for women. Women were encouraged to enter certain scientific and technical fields such as gynaecology, pharmacology, midwifery and the laboratory work etc. The regime had to compromise women's exclusion from judgeship to accept them into this position though in a limited capacity. In 1992, a law allowed women to sit as assistant judges in courts hearing divorce cases. The 1992 Family law made it mandatory that marriage contract can list stipulations under which women can initiate divorce. Family planning programmes were encouraged by the government.

The 1990s was thus characterized by a quiet kind of a revolt by women and included many innovative and entrepreneurial characteristics of women's activism and included the publication of many feminist magazines (*Zanan, Farzaneh, Jens-e Dovvom* etc). These magazines criticized the subordinate status of women in the Islamic Republic and called for modernizing the family law; academicians forming women's studies courses or programs at the universities, the growth of NGO'S devoted to women's empowerment, and the emergence of Islamic feminism whereby women sought to frame their demands for their rights in religious idioms and to recover their religion from patriarchal interpretations.

Women votes were crucial to the election of President Mohammad Khatami in 1997 and then again in 2001. The Khatami years saw the growth and vitality of Iranian civil society and a movement for political and cultural reform. In 1997 for the first time a woman was appointed as a judge after the establishment of Islamic Republic. Women's *mehrieh* became exempted from the taxes. Growing proportions of public sector employees were women in the Ministry of health and education. There was more tolerance for professional women and many women were appointed to the managerial position. The Tehran Bureau of Education announced in 2000 that elementary school students were allowed to wear "happy, bright colours", in place of traditional black. In the academic year 2002-2003 women's university enrolments exceeded those of men for the first time since universities were established in Iran. In 2002, single women received permission to study abroad on government fellowships. Numerous women's organizations, bureaus, offices and commissions are also formed; each year these groups organize many seminars, conferences etc on various women's issues. In 2004, the number of women athletes was estimated around more than 1.2 million. [2]

Despite a reformist decade legal framework remained very unfavourable for women. Women still faced numerous discriminatory policies and practices. For example, forced veiling subjects women to harsh penalties for non-compliance. Women still needed father's legal permission to get married. Father still has the exclusive right of child custody in case of divorce. Inheritance law still favours men. Child marriage and legal sanction of violence against women in the form of honour killing solidified men's prerogatives over women. The provisions of *Ghesas*, the Law of Retribution in which the value of a woman's life is calculated as the blood money *(Diyeh)* payable to the family of the victim for a wrongful death is half that charged for the death of a man (Article 258).

In the run up to the elections of 2005, feminists mobilized to take the call for women's equality in the family and the society to the streets. For the first time since 1979, public protest by women took place in March and June 2005 and 2006. Feminists in Iran were openly demanding equality in family issues, an end to stoning as a punishment for real sexual transgression, and the ratification of the UN's Convention of all Forms of Discrimination against women (CEDAW) along with the abrogation of all gender discriminatory laws in Iran.

But after the election of Mahmoud Ahmadinejad the authorities launched a crackdown on feminist protest. Women protestors were arrested, jailed, and charged with undermining state security. State repression forced the women's movement to devise a new strategy in 2006 for legal and policy change: the One Million Signature petition campaign. This is a door-to-door campaign to obtain signatures for the abrogation of all discriminatory laws and provide women with equality in home and in society. In 2007, the judiciary introduced a new prenuptial agreement that conditioned the payment of mehrieh upon men's financial ability. The Ahmadinejad government extolled a greater resort to polygamy as a solution to pervasive female unemployment. In January 2008, the authorities closed down the veteran women's magazine *Zanan*. Along with this in December 2008, the Parliament finally granted the right to inherit land from their deceased husbands.

There have been significant improvements in the women's education and health along with a remarkable drop in the birth rates. Hence, the policies of the Islamist Government cannot be categorized as being totally disadvantageous for women. Thus, the popular notion that Islamism has enforced a harsh form of sexual repression on the Iranian women does not convey the complexity of what has taken place.

Hence, the question arises that how can such important reforms, which have many positive implications for women, coexist with misogynist laws and policies? The various chapters in the thesis partly answer this question by examining the nature of Iranian polity, role of Islam, nature of women's movement and the nature of *ulema's* factional politics in Iran.

Chapter 1 focuses on the linkage between gender, state and religion, and how state uses gender and religion for legitimization its own policies as well as for the construction of nation. The chapter also highlights historical linkage between religion and division of power between the genders. It also addresses the issue related to patriarchy, politics of recognition, sexuality, culture and social movements and how the same affects gender discourse in the context of Iran.

Chapter 2 focuses on the Islamic gender ideology with special reference to Imam Khomeini's ideas, Constitutional status of women in post revolutionary Iran along with the various policies of the state in marriage, divorce, child custody, family planning, education, employment and its impact on Iranian women. The linkage between the ideology of Imam Khomeini and constitutional articles related to women has also been highlighted.

Chapters 3 and 4 concern the exploration of the policies of the three Presidents (Rafsanjani, Khatami and Ahmadinejad) towards the Iranian women. The linkage between the broad Islamic orientation, socio-economic policies of these governments and their policy orientation towards women has been stressed upon. It focuses on how the second decade saw the emergence of new leadership, policy shifts, and changing societal expectations in the context of the program for economic liberalization and integration into global economy as well the liberalizing thrust of state policies towards women. The fourth chapter reflects upon the regressive policies of Ahmadinejad government towards Iranian women.

Chapter 5 primarily analyzes the nature of women movements, its leaderships, its heterogeneous character, its method of mobilization and influencing the government machinery, its limitations and success in the post-Khomeini period. It highlights the various responses of the different women groups under different governments and the socio-economic conditions to the policies of different Islamic regimes.

Chapter 6 reflects the broad findings of this study and indicates the role of gendering politics in the reduction of power-gap between genders, if not the emergence of gender friendly or gender neutral nation- building process. In addition, the conclusion captures the various trends related to women movement that emerged since 1989.

Endnotes

1. Shahidian, Hammed (2002), "Gender Politics in Islamic Republic" p. 163, Greenwood Press, London.
2. Afary, Janet (2009), "Sexual Politics in Iran", p. 333, Cambridge University Press.

New Delhi **Jyotika Teckchandani**

Acknowledgements

This book is the result of a challenging journey, of six years in which many people have contributed and given their support.

To begin with, I would like to thank the exemplary women of Iran whose continuous struggle for the gender justice inspired me to explore complex power relationship that impinges and surrounds the everyday struggle for women in this modern world. These strong, empowering women encouraged me to take up this research work on the most challenging and emerging field of gender politics.

I owe a special debt of gratitude to the Iranian students/nationals whom I met during the course of my research in Delhi. Thank you for sharing your lives with me. I can never justly recognize them by mere acknowledgement. This book would have been impossible without their opinions, ideas, stories and experiences.

This book is a tribute to my family for their continuous love and support. Words cannot express my gratitude for my parents. They selflessly encouraged me to explore new directions in life and instilled in me the determination to fulfil my dreams. Thank you Mummy and Papa for your unconditional love, patience and for all the sacrifices that you have made for me. Your prayer for me has what sustained me so far.

I am grateful to my sister, Hansika for always being there for me, giving me the much needed strength and for helping me sail through the myriad challenges. Thank you for your suggestions, feedback, assistance, love and for always showing me the right path in life.

Also, I would like to thank my brother-in-law Puneet for boosting my morale throughout the course of this study. He has always been a source of optimism and constant motivation. A special thanks to my two and half year old nephew Shaurya, who has brought immeasurable joy in my life.

Big thanks to my friend Jasmeet for always listening to my vague ideas patiently. I would also like to take this opportunity to thank my Soka friends Anshu Narayan Sharma for helping me believe in my potential and Dipika Jain for standing with me during the most vulnerable moments of my life.

Finally, I am extremely thankful to Mr. Sandeep Sury, CEO of New Century Publications, for showing great interest in my work and bringing it out in the public domain for wider academic discussion.

I would like to dedicate this book to my mentor Dr. Daisaku Ikeda....Sensei, thank you for reminding me during these six years, "If winter comes, can spring be far behind?" Sensei, I have lived your guidance every day....

Thank you for everything!!

This is for you Sensei.......

1

Matrix of Gender, State, Nation and Religion: Theoretical Framework

1.1 Gender Defined

Gender refers to the cultural ideas that normatively order images and expectations on the basis of socially defined masculinity and feminity. Gender plays a pivotal role in the ordering of the society through various forms of gendering, refashioning of structures of patriarchy, contestation over gender roles and struggle over sexuality and its use as an identity marker for the collective. As Judith Lorber puts it, gender is "a process of social construction, a system of social stratification and an institution that structures every aspect of our lives because of its embedment in the family, the workplace, and the state as well as in sexuality, language and culture". [1]

Social identification of sexes is important primarily because it reflects how a society construes and constructs sex and gender. Gender relations and the meaning of gender identity change in accordance with changes in access of men and women to various social resources. Gender, as Butler has argued is neither an essence nor an objective, external ideal to accomplish; it is, rather performative that is, created by the very acts of gender. Gender is a construction that regularly conceals its genesis. [2] Because of its contingent, relational nature, gender is not always acted out consistently; socially acceptable gender identity is never fully attained. Socially defined gender denotes power as central to making gender relations and identities. Power operates through multiple mechanisms and is never completely unidirectional. [3] In interaction between the sexes the power is often negotiated through the articulation of specific gender definitions.

Gender does not only refer to what men and women are biologically but, to the ideological (or discursive) and material relations also that exist between groups of people called 'men' and people called 'women'. The terms 'masculine' and 'feminine' do not describe natural characteristics but are gender terms. In all societies and in all cultures there are emotional and psychological characteristics that are held to be essentially male or female. Similarly, when sex and gender do not coincide naturally, individuals who are born as males and females are usually expected to develop masculine or feminine character traits and behave in ways appropriate to their gender. Like for example, women are considered to be more passive, emotional and sensitive than men and that men by contrast are considered more aggressive, rational and logical. This notion has been used to justify gender inequality and female subordination to male authority. Feminists have pointed out that rather than reflecting the personality traits of men and women, ideas about gender have been used to justify unequal treatment and thus provided an important ideological justification for a specific form of social inequality. [4]

The view of gender as social and not natural points to the importance of discursive constructions or inter-subjective understanding of gender, that is, the social meaning and significance attributed to perceived sex differences. Gender is material in a sense that even while one's gender is not necessarily rooted in the materiality of ones sexed body, it is nevertheless embedded in social institutions and practices that reproduce gender identities, gender roles and gender relations. Hence, in any society one's gender will influence one's entitlement to concrete resources and will be a crucial factor in deciding who gets what, but also who can do what one is permitted to 'be' in any given society. [5] Thus, Gender also intertwines with class, ethnicity, race, sexual orientations, beliefs and ideological commitments.

1.2 Religion, Gender and Sexuality

Sexuality is one of the most powerful dimensions of

individual and inter-subjective human life. The act of sexual intercourse between two consulting adults is not only a source of erotic pleasure but also creates a lifelong emotional bond with a potential to beget a new life and reproduce kinship structures and social reproduction. For this reason sexuality is considered the most intimate expression of the embodied self the most private of affairs and the primary source of socio-biological reproduction and therefore a public affair which no society can leave unregulated. [6]

Religions are discursive systems of beliefs and practices [7] that offer structures of moral order, meaning weaving discourse of life through means of transcendental communication with divine reality. Religions have historically been involved in the regulation of sexuality, biological and social reproduction, and family structure and gender relations on the basis of its transcendental principle as natural, sacred or of divine origin. The industrialization of economy and modern democratic value system has brought a fundamental transformation in the conception of sexual orientation, gender relations and gender roles that is threatening the epistemological foundation of all religious traditions, particularly the monotheistic religious traditions. Thus, almost all religions are opposed to homosexual or uni-sexual marriage. It is not without reason that many scholars see the Islamic revolution as a brutal, patriarchal attempt to control the increasing assertion of sexual freedom of Iranian women. [8] In fact it is not surprising that many analysts see the resurgence of religious "fundamentalism" at global level primarily as a patriarchal reaction to the growing worldwide assertion of gender equality and feminism. [9]

In this context patriarchy, as Walby suggests, underwent a series of modifications in the past two centuries partly in response to women's demands for equal status in society, and partly in response to increase the control of the state over all aspects of social life. [10] In the area of employment women were no longer barred from certain professions; they were instead confined to jobs segregated from and valued less than those of men. The exclusion of women from political and cultural realms has been replaced by their subordination.

Thus, the control over female sexuality has shifted from the exclusive control of father, husband or brother to that of a broader public arena. In public patriarchy, the expropriation of women has been effected more collectively than by individual patriarchs. The shift in the site of sexual domination from private to public is accompanied by a change in patriarchal strategy from exclusion to segregation and subordination whereby women are no longer barred from economic, cultural, and political institutions, but their domains of their involvement are segregated from and graded lower than those of men. [11] Gender or the 'Woman question' has become in this respect the pre-eminently contested "social question", while "religion" has been thrown, willingly or unwillingly, into the vortex of the global contestation. [12]

In order to structure the relationship between the gender, sexuality and religion Birgit Heller [13] provides an useful tripartite analytical differentiation between: (a) the issue of women's status and roles in different religious traditions, that is, the kinds of institutionalized gendered religious division of labour within particular religious regimes; (b) the subject of cultural images, ideas, stereotypes and norms about women within diverse discursive religious traditions; and (c) the question what women as religious subjects do and think.

1.2.1 Gendered Religious Division of Labour and Power Relations within Religious Regimes: Sociologically speaking, one can understand the institutionalized religions as religious regimes having a system of production, consumptions, and distribution of power, authority, and decision making within a community in relation to what is considered the 'sacred' good, In this context one relevant question that arises here pertains to access and share of specific gender in the system of production, distribution and consumption of religious goods. [14] In other words how gendered is the distribution of symbolic power and resources in a religious regime? Though all monotheistic religions including Islam treat believer equally irrespective of gender and they are all equal in the eyes of God. Casanova has rightly noted that, "God is the source and model of equitable justice and fairness to all. Moreover, as 'the most Merciful and Compassionate', God is considered to look after for the weak, the poor, the meek, the orphan, the widow etc. This is the core prophetic ethical norm that anticipates modern gendered equality as a transcendent principle". [15]

However, notwithstanding the notion of equality, fairness and justice being the integral part of all monotheistic religions, the institutionalized religious system everywhere in its operational reality is characterized by unequal access to divine knowledge and distribution of divine resources. With the passage of time as the religious systems became routinized it acquired the patriarchal values as the basic principles of religion. One consequence of this process is the gradual development of unequal access along gender and class line to religious resources.

Thus the priesthood in the case of the Catholic Church, and to some extent the *Ulama* [16] in the case of Islam, as hierarchically differentiated and high status religious roles, is exclusively male, [17] though female assertion in this role is emerging. Further, though Islam paid special importance to equality to gender and individual women had close access to Prophet Muhammad and played important roles in the history of Islam, however the later development of institutionalized Islamic tradition did marginalize the status of women in Muslim societies.

In the specific context of Iranian *Shi'i* Islam where there did develop a highly differentiated and hierarchically organized structure [18] but there is hardly any women *ayatollah or hojatoleslam* in the Iranian society. The issue of representation of women in the ulema class is increasing. Amina Wadud, in the United States even led the mixed gender *namaz* congregation with her being the Imam. [19] In this context, pious veiled Muslim women becoming ever more visible in the public sphere of Muslim societies and increasingly attending mosque services can be interpreted actually as a sign of increasing religious gendered equality, and thus as evidence of the modernization of Islam under the pressure of modern gender democracy rather than as a fundamentalist reaction to modernity. [20] In this respect, it can be read as evidence of the pressure of global secular norms upon all religious traditions.

This raises a fundamental question with regard to the proper boundary between the private and public or between religious and secular spheres. Though modernity has sharpened the private/public dichotomy, the boundary between the two is historically and culturally contingent, fuzzy in nature and therefore has been open to continuous public contestation and redrawing. Thus what is considered 'private' under secular dispensation might appear to be 'public' from religious point of view. For instance 'sexual morality' is strictly a private affair under secular order but for religious people it is a 'public' matter. Thus, the public debates surrounding over abortion, conversion, blasphemy, multiculturalism, polygamy, women rights, lesbian and gay rights do not allow for simple, straightforward, uncontroversial answers but rather varies from society to society. For the same reasons many aspects connected with universal human rights are subject to sharp religious and cultural contestation.

1.2.2 Religion and Sexism: Representation of Women in Religious Traditions: The issue of relationship between religion and sexuality concerns the issue of representation of women in religious tradition. Therefore it is important to find out how women have been represented in Islamic tradition. Historically speaking, *Qur'an* is gender neutral and speaks equality of sexes in clear terms. Today there is an intense debate among Muslim intelligentsia including *ulema* concerning the proper representation of women within Islam. While there is an emerging consensus about the marginalized position of women in Muslim society, there is a less consensus whether Islam had any role in legitimating the gender inequality within Muslim societies. The dominant Muslim intelligentsia tends to blame the conservative role of *Ulema* and misrepresentation of Islamic traditions. However, there is an emerging minority view that argues that the Prophetic Revelation and the *Sunnah* of the Prophet did not constitute an improvement in the situation of women when compared with the reigning conditions in the immediate pre-Islamic period in the Arabian Peninsula. [21]

It is more widely accepted that Muhammad himself respected and trusted women and tried to provide for equal participation of women in the religious life of the *ummah*. [22] On the other hand, there is evidence for a rapid decline with the institutionalization of the early Muslim community, marked by what Jane Smith has termed a dual process of "exclusion" and "seclusion", that is, the exclusion of women not only from leadership roles but also from the communal aspects of religious life and their seclusion to a place apart from normal social intercourse with men. [23]

In this regard the most heated controversies are about the role of veiling as a marker and assertion of Muslim identity in the increasingly globalized world. Veiling, above all, has become the most salient, contested, and controversial emblem of contemporary global Islam. As Nilüfer Göle has pointed out, "no other symbol than the veil reconstructs with such a force the 'otherness' of Islam to the West. Women's bodies and sexuality reappear as a political site of difference and resistance to the homogenizing and egalitarian forces of Western modernity". [24]

Although in the Western imagination, the "headscarf" signifies the subordination of women in the Muslim society. Though in part this reflects the western sensibility of notion of equality, but in part also functions as marker of differentiation from Muslim society. Thus, one finds a plethora of works that have questioned such a simplistic liberal, feminist and secularist reading of the phenomenon of veiling in the Muslim societies and offer a more nuanced, ambivalent, and contextual interpretations. [25] Indeed, throughout the Muslim world, particularly in the Middle East including Iran, the veil has functioned as power enabling the Muslim women to participate in the public sphere with greater freedom and assertion, a marker of Muslim subjectivity and cultural authenticity and differentiation from other civilization.

However, notwithstanding the 'thrust of equality' embedded in the narratives of Great Textual Tradition, the vernacularization of almost all religious texts and traditions has resulted in making women and the family a crucial symbolic factor in constructing group solidarity vis-à-vis wider society in most of religious traditions. [26] Under such conditions, women's behaviour and conducts becomes a symbol of group integrity. This partly explains the dominant representation of women in all religious traditions as mothers, caregivers, educators, and moral guardians and gradual transformation of women as inviolable repository of 'authentic' group identity. This valorization occurs through carefully crafted binary codes of 'respectable' behaviour: the female group member ought to be veiled (versus exposed), modest (versus promiscuous), loyal (versus morally corrupt), married (versus sexualized), fertile (versus childless), and so on. [27]

Thus in the Islamic Republic of Iran (IRI), and in other Muslim countries, heterosexuality is considered as the proper gender behaviour and all other kinds of sexual orientations, behaviour or relations are either banned or criminalized. Only heterosexuality can reproduce and regulate the nation in all Muslim societies including Islamic Republic of Iran. [28]

1.2.3 Women as Religious Subjects, Historical Agents, and Political Actors: The proliferation of feminist religious discourses in recent years reflects a desire of women for radical transformations in religious traditions in order to achieve the goal of equity and justice. Islam is no exception to this emerging trend as evident for the proliferation of Islamic feminist writings. [29] At the same time, these attempts of feminist writings to restructure the religious politics of gender have evoked sharp internal contestations and debates. [30]

Certainly in recent years in the Muslim societies, a good number of women has embarked on reading and understanding the sacred texts without the mediation, interpretation, and control of male religious authorities, which indicates a first hermeneutics step on the road to female religious subjectivity and agency. It is on this complex relation between gender, morality, religion, feminism and secularization that one can observe very different dynamics throughout the Muslim world. Indeed, as Saba Mahmood has pointed out, "the vexing relationship between feminism and religion is perhaps most manifest in discussions of Islam". [31] Muslim women not only have entered the mosque, but are in many cases leaders of the modern mosque movement, thereby challenging the traditional image of the mosque, and the *ummah,* as a public male assembly. [32] Further, the female veil is becoming the public face of global Islam.

It is precisely this public manifestation of female agency and subjectivity and the grassroots character of the mass movement that baffles liberal and secular feminist assumptions as well as our conceptions of a modern civil society. As Mahmood has asked rhetorically: "why would such a large number of women across the Muslim world actively support a movement that seems inimical to their 'own interests and agendas,' especially at a historical moment when these women appear to have more emancipatory possibilities available to them"? [33] The fact that the movement also enjoys support from highly educated and articulated women from the upper and middle-income strata of many Muslim societies, makes explanations in terms of "false consciousness" "self-imposed tutelage" or the "feminist intuition" that women (like men) can internalize norms that lead to their own oppression, even more problematic. [34]

1.3 Relationship between Gender, Nation and State

Feminist scholars Nira-Yuval Davis [35], Floya Anthias [36] and Jill Steans [37] have shown the relevance of gender relations in the construction of the nation and underlined the significance of women, sexuality and the family as symbols in the reproduction of the nation and its boundaries. It is not uncommon to find out that the nation is depicted as woman. The deeply ingrained image of homeland as a female body whose violations by foreigners require citizens to rush to her defence is a powerful image in nationalist ideology. This depends upon the image of woman as chaste and dutiful. Not only the nationalism is couched in terms of love of country but also within this imaging of the nation, women, serve as the repository of group identity. National identity is equated with ideas about gender, parentage and skin colour. Women not only bear the burden of being the mothers of the nation but their bodies may also be used to reproduce the boundaries of the national group, transmit its culture and become the privileged signifiers of national difference. [38]

The power of nation lies in its appeal to a sense of belonging of being at home. The identification of women with the private domain of the home and family reinforces the powerful imagery of a national community with that of the selfless/devoted mother. [39] This automatically triggers response that one should be ready to sacrifice himself or herself in defence of her chastity and honour. The symbolic connection between the idea of woman and the idea of nation and the use of women as symbols of nations by nationalist and liberationist movements has been critical to the gendering of women's membership in national communities. Despite the diversity of identities and loyalties in any specific nation, the ideal of 'woman' has fuelled the ideals of 'authentic' national cultures, 'indigenous' religions, 'traditional' family forms. The category of 'woman', as a stand-in for 'nation, 'has been marketed to delineate 'national' boundaries. [40]

Such usage of 'woman' has gone hand in hand with the

imposition of forms of behavioural control on women in the name of the nation, in the name of liberation, in the name of progress, and in the name of God. Thus, the Nations, seen as imagined communities, to use Anderson phrase, [41] use "the woman" as a critical symbol in inventing their notions of themselves.

The metamorphization of nation as women is grounded in patriarchal relationships. Consequently, the female body becomes the battleground not only for countries and their enemies, but also for competing definitions of" national identity. [42] Preserving a pure national identity becomes equivalent to protecting and controlling women's sexuality. [43] Control of women's sexuality has become a core of the power struggle between the ideologically rival groups in the political system. The state has played an important role in modifying and restructuring gender relations and women's sexuality. Thus, in its attempt to Islamize the women's position, the IRI resorted to coercion, passed in-egalitarian laws and mobilized female morality squads to enforce its codes of propriety in order to imagine its own version of Islamic nation. [44]

The family constituted the basis of society in which the women played the most important role as mothers. Women were regarded as transmitters of communal and national values to their next generation. As a result the preservation of the status quo and the change were linked to the position of women. Women were constructed as reproducers of communal, national and religious identity. [45] Women's behaviour, clothing, patterns of reproduction, life style and ways of thinking were all regarded as symbols of communal identity and markers of national boundaries.

The above linkage between gender and nation is mediated through the administrative agency of state. As the identity of nation is far from settled in most of societies, particularly in post- colonial societies, it is the state that fashion and refashions the construction of nation building in the societies.

It is in the process of nation-building that state differentially impacts on the gender relationship in the society depending upon its ideological world view, social base and nature of factional politics. Further most of the state policies are justified in the name of 'national interest' or to build a powerful nation. In this sense nation emerges as modern legitimizing category for contraction and expansion of gender specific rights depending upon the context.

States intervene in women's lives for the purpose of internal and external policy. Internationally, the state uses women and their portrayal as westernized and Islamized, veiled or unveiled in order to depict a distinct political identity and message abroad. Domestically, whether weak or strong, secular or religious the political regime manipulates women's sexuality and their labour in order to legitimize its cultural and political position and to consolidate its power. Depending upon the ideological propensities and material social base state unleashes the programme for expanding or contracting gender specific opportunity structure. In the process state sets an agenda for the control of particular class of women or their activities. It builds alliances with different classes of women especially in their policies of mobilization. Gender can have a huge influence in policy making and functioning of the State. Gender remains a core concern of politics. Gender analysis illuminates politics and power struggle: who gets what, when, how and why. [46]

The state has no fixed relationship to the gender; it is evolving, dialectic and dynamic [47] because the state is not a single-minded actor with a unified set of interests. States are composed of different, conflicting, and changing sets of interests. The state, in fact, is a contested terrain, its actions reflects local, national, and global conflicts and contradictions. The state policies construct men and women differently. Women on the one hand are constructed like men as citizens. But they are also treated a special category in relation to various roles they play in society. Women are assigned status as mothers and revered as symbols of national and communal identity. [48] Rights and responsibilities of the women are often defined by the state. The state therefore partly reflects and creates particular forms of gender inequality and gender relations. Gendered identities are in part constructed by the law and public discourses, which emanate from the state.

Although the state has the ability to modify and reshape gender relations and women's lives but at times its actions are also shaped by the persistence of women's resistance. As active and reactive agents of social change, women respond to and defy state actions. Women pose challenges to the system, sometimes successfully, sometimes not. [49] Women's responses vary historically; it varies not only by their class background, ideological dispositions, and religious outlook, but also by the degree of their political and feminist awareness and how well they can articulate their interests and issues of their concerns.

As Shirin Rai [50] argues that the relationship between the state and gender is not fixed and immutable, battles can be fought out in the arena of the state. Consequently, the state has for most part acted to reinforce female subordination; the space can exist within the state to act to change gender relation. Women's relationship to the state can also be seen as a site of contestation which provides the context for mobilization, and the state can function as a locus of resistance. The policies of the state and their impact on women are generally divided into three major categories. The first set is the policies which are aimed fundamentally at women. These often focus the so called protective legislation and reproduction, e.g. abortion laws and laws surroundings childbirth such as provision of maternity leave.

A second subdivision is those policies which refer to the relation between men and women, particularly property rights, family relations, labour laws, areas where power relations between men and women are and therefore set off gender relations are often institutionalized. The law and regulation surrounding these issues become an area of contestation when attempts are made to alter the existing pattern of power relationships as occurred and women's mobility become highly contested. The third set of policies—general and gender neutral—have and different impact on women and men. This involves the developmental programme of the government such as setting up industry , communication, transportation, Defence, law and order machinery, education etc. that are conceived in gender-neutral framework but have differential impact on gender. [51]

1.4 Gender, Islam and State in Iran

It is within the above theoretical formulation that the issue of relationship between gender, Islam and state in post revolutionary Iran has been analyzed in the following chapters of the thesis. The duality of Iranian political structure further complicates the analysis of gender relationship in post-revolutionary Iran. Notwithstanding the limitation of dual structure, the key to understanding the gender discourse in Islamic Republic of Iran is interpretative field of Islam that legitimizes and delegitimizes various actions of state including its gender related programme and policies.

Women's issues in Iran became all the more important because Iranian society in this period underwent a rare historical moment, a moment of revolution and of restructuring of state and society in the aftermath of revolution. It was during this period that various principles and organs of Islamic state in Iran were institutionalized under the supervision of late Imam Khomeini, the founder of Islamic Republic of Iran. Women affected the national processes in the same way as much they were affected by them.

The Islamic state's mission has been to create an ideal Islamic society wherein women and men can accomplish their holy duties. As the family is regarded as the microcosm of society IRI has considered it pivotal to 'strengthen the family' that is, to emphasize the primacy of the women's domestic roles and to secure men's position as the head of the household. In the Islamic state, individuals ought to belong to 'right' gender and must have the 'right gender interaction'. Gender and politics become inter-wined: correct politics creates correct gender and correct gender increases one's chances in the social and the political arenas. [52]

The prominent place given to the women and family in the Constitution of IRI reflected the depth of interest expressed by all competing ideologies in the relationship between the gender and nation. The Constitution clearly demonstrated that the Islamic nation was dependent on the Islamization of gender relations. It constructed a new 'Islamic' link between nation and gender and specified a corresponding position for women. Women were constructed as citizens in the interest of the nation building, but they were also defined in their special roles within the state and community. Women were defined as biological reproducers of the community and nation and were assigned roles on this basis.

In the post-revolutionary Iran, the authorities explicitly define the parameters of gender appearances. The law prohibits a range of gender-inappropriate behaviours (e.g.; long hair for men, unladylike comportment for women) and deviant clothes like see-through, short scarves that do not completely cover hair and neck, anklets, sunglasses. [53] Control of women's sexuality is viewed to be another aim of the Islamic state. As Fatima Mernissi has noted that the sexual power attributed to women has caused the Islamic states to contain and control their sexuality through such social institutions such as the veil, the family, the marriage system and the legal system. [54]

The Islamists came to power following the decades of refashioning patriarchy that afforded women greater freedom and mobility and curbed men's power within the family. The IRI has sought to reinforce male dominance within the family, reinstate men's prerogative compromised under the Pahlavi's, and define women primarily in their private roles of wife and mother. Women's social role in the pre revolutionary Iran has made it impossible to send women back to their homes. Though successful in passing legislation that limit's women options, state has been forced to accept women's limited public presence, so as long as it did not interfere with their familial duties.

The discourse on gender relations in post-revolutionary Iran is very complex and cuts the dominant binary framework of tradition vs. modernity. The thrust of state-mediated gender discourse have been marked by contradictory pulls and pressures of confining the dominant role of women to private sphere while offering the limited role in political-public sphere. The Islamic Republic did not inherit a ready- made Islamic policy on gender. The dominant conceptions of gender were constructed as events developed in post-revolutionary society. Thus, the gender relations in IRI can also be understood in terms of conflictual between conservative *ulema* who opt for larger domestication of women and the progressive ulema who fight to safeguard and expand their rights. Hence, the variations within Islamic interpretation over the role of gender must be taken into consideration while analyzing the relationship between gender and state in post-revolutionary Iran.

Endnotes

1. Lorber, Judith (1994), "Paradoxes of Gender", p. 5, New Haven, CT: Yale Press.
2. Butler, Judith (1990), "Gender Trouble: Feminism and the Subversion of Identity", p. 140, New York: Routledge.
3. Shahidian, Hammed (2002), "Gender Politics in Islamic Republic", p. 5, Greenwood Press, London.
4. Steans, Jill (2006), "Gender and International Relations", p. 9, Polity Press.
5. Ibid., 8.
6. Casanova, Jose, "Religion, Politics and Gender Equality in Public Religions Revisited", p. 15, available at: www.unrisd.org/80256B3C005BCCF9/.../$file/WEBCasvadrftII pdf.
7. See for details, Assad, Talal (1993), "Genealogies of Religion: Discipline and Reasons of Power in Christianity and Islam",

Baltimore: The John Hopkins University Press.

8. For details see Fathi, Asghar (1997), "Women and the Family in Iran", Brill Academic Publishers; Moallem, Minoo (2005), "Between Warrior Brother and Veiled Sister: Islamic Fundamentalism and the Politics of Patriarchy in Iran", University of California Press.
9. Riesebrodt, Martin (1998), "Pious Passion: The Emergence of Modern Fundamentalism in the United States and Iran", Berkeley, CA: University of California Press.
10. Walby, Sylvia (1994), "Theorizing Patriarchy", p. 179, Cambridge, MA: Blackwell.
11. Ibid.,179.
12. Casanova, No. 6, p. 16.
13. The classification has been taken from Casanova, Jose, No. 6. Citing Birgit, Heller. 'Gender and Religion', in Børresen Kari Elisabeth (ed). (2001), "Gender and Religion", pp. 357-359, Roma: Carocci editore.
14. Ibid.
15. Ibid.
16. *Ulama* (singular *alim)* does not constitute a pristly class in Muslim society, as there is no Church in Islam. However, as Ulema came to identify themselves as custodian of Prophetic traditions and carries the main responsibility to convey the correct message of Prophet (*dawa*), they have functioned as clerical class.
17. Casanova, No. 6, p. 18.
18. Ibid.
19. Wadud, Amina, a Professor in the USA led the mixed gender Friday prayer in a mosque of New York in 2005. See 'Woman leads US Muslims to prayer', available at: http://news.bbc.co.uk/2/hi/americas/4361931.stm.
20. Casanova, No. 6, p. 19.
21. For details see Ahmed, Leila (1992), "Women and Gender in Islam: Historical Roots of Modern Debate", New Haven: Yale University Press; Stowasser, Barbara Freyer (1994), "Women in the Qur'an, Traditions, and Interpretation", New York: Oxford University Press; Wadud, Amina (1999), "Qur'an and Woman: Re-Reading the Sacred Text from a Woman's Perspective", New York: Oxford University Press.
22. Ibid.

23. For details see Smith, Jane I., "Women, Religion and Social Change in Early Islam", in Yvonne Yazbeck Haddad and Ellison Banks Findly (ed.) (1985), 'Women, Religion, and Social Change', pp. 19-31, Albany: SUNY Press.
24. This has been taken from Casonova, No.6., citing Göle, Nilüfer. "The Forbidden Modern Civilization and Veiling", 1995, p. 1, Ann Arbor: The University of Michigan Press.
25. See, Mahmood, Saba (2005), "Politics of Piety: The Islamic Revival and the Feminist Subject", Princeton: Princeton University Press. Also, Hosseini, Ziba Mir (1999), "Islam and Gender: The Religious Debate in Contemporary Islam", Princeton: Princeton University Press.
26. Some of good literature on this subject matter is Shachar, Ayelet (2001), "Multicultural Jurisdictions: Cultural Differences and Women's Rights", pp. 45-62, Cambridge: Cambridge University Press. Kandiyoti, Deniz (ed.) (1991), 'Women, Islam and State', London: Macmillan Press.
27. Shachar, Ayelet, "Religion, State, and the Problem of Gender: New Modes of Citizenship and Governance in Diverse Societies", p. 3, available at: lawjournal.mcgill.ca/userfiles/other/410530-1225240850_Shachar.pdf.
28. Shahidian, No. 3, p. 9.
29. Casanova, No. 6, p. 24.
30. Ibid.
31. Mahmood, No. 25, p. 1.
32. Wadud, No. 19.
33. Mahmood, No. 25, p. 2.
34. Casanova, No. 6, p. 28.
35. See Davis, Nira Yuval and Floya, Anthias (eds.) (1989), "Woman-Nation-State. London: Macmillan.
36. Ibid.
37. Steans, No. 4, p. 3.
38. For the above paragraph, see Ibid., 40.
39. For details see Steans, No. 4, p. 55.
40. Joseph, Suad, "Gender and Citizenship in the Arab World", available at: http://iwsaw.lau.edu.lb/publications/al-raida/citizenship-and-gender-in-the.php.
41. Anderson, Benedict (2007), "Imagined Communities:

Reflections on the Origin and Spread of Nationalism", Verso Books.

42. Shahidian, No. 3, p. 19.
43. Ibid.
44. Ibid.
45. See Davis, Nira Yuval and Floya, Anthias, No. 35, p. 7.
46. For the above paragraph see Sedghi, Hamideh (2007), "Women and Politics in Iran: Veiling, Unveiling, and Reveiling", pp. 2-8, Cambridge University Press.
47. For the above paragraph see Waylen, Georgina, "Analysing Women in Third World Politics", in Haleh Afsar, "Women and Politics in Third World", 1996 (ed.), p. 15, Routledge.
48. Paider, Parvin (1995), "Women and the Political Process in Twentieth Century Iran", p. 22, Cambridge: Cambridge University Press.
49. Sedghi, No. 46, p. 4.
50. Rai, Shirin, (1996), "Women and the State in the Third World", in Haleh Afsar (ed.),' Women and Politics in Third World', p. 13, Routledge.
51. For the above paragraph see Waylen, No. 47, p. 13.
52. For the above paragraph see Shahidian, No. 3, p. 213.
53. Ibid., pp. 166-170.
54. Mernissi, Fatima (1975), "Beyond the Veil: Male-Female Dynamics in a Modern Muslim Society", pp. xv, second edition, Bloomington: Indiana University Press.

2

Imam Khomeini and Iran: Implications for Iranian Women

2.1 Introduction

As demonstrated by previous chapter gender is a volatile site for the 'politics of construction of nation'. Women emerge as a marker for evaluating the modernizing as well as conservative policies of a given polity. The Pahlavi regime in Iran was hailed by the West as 'modernizing monarch' for its approach and policies on women that included granting a vote to women, more liberalized life style and more public visibility of women. On the contrary, the non-modernized social and political forces, particularly the *Ulema*, looked at Shah's modernization programme primarily as having corrupting influence on Iranian society. Since this chapter attempts to explore the impact of Imam Khomeini's thought in construction of Islamic republic and its implications for Iranian women, it is worthwhile first to examine his views and ideas about women in order to delineate his impact on the construction of Islamic Republic of Iran and its policies and programmes enunciated from time to time towards the Iranian women.

Ayatollah Ruhollah Musavi Khomeini (1902-1989), the architect of Islamic revolution in Iran, view the issue of the status and position of women in a Muslim society through a prism of his understanding of Islam and Islamic history which was relatively more political in approach and orientation. In accordance with this understanding, Khomeini rejected the Western-materialistic perspective of development and life process as well as (mechanical) equality of sexes. He holds that Islam has liberated the mankind including women from the period of *Jahiliyya* (The Age of Darkness—before the period of origin Islam and) and restore them equality, freedom and dignity. According to him, Islam clearly defined the rights (social, political and economic) and duties of women and man and any undue interference with divinely mandated rights, duties, obligations and commandments would not only jeopardize the healthy man-women relationship but would also harm the Islamic societies and nation.

In the Islamic prescription of life process, God is the creator, lawmaker and judge. [1] He has a predefined order. Men and women have distinct responsibilities, corresponding to their nature. They do not make manhood and womanhood; they strive towards these already made identities. Hence, gender is not made-it is teleological. [2] This teleological system assigns men and women distinct but complimentary roles.

Since for Khomeini and many other *Ulema*, a healthy Muslim society must be gender segregated which does not mean inequality as it is popularly understood. Khomeini's opposed modernizing and secularizing reform of the Pahlavi Shah as this will affect the God's ordained relationship between men and women as well as to protect the *Ulema's* interest. Having abolished the monarchy he shaped the Constitution of Islamic Republic and organs of the State in a manner that conform, as far as possible, to his imagination of Iranian nation in which men and women could live their life as per Islamic injunctions and fully utilize their role, strength and aspirations for the betterment of Iranian society and nation.

Ayatollah Khomeini had strong misgivings about the modernizing reform of the Shah, particularly the reform pertaining to women and considered the 'liberalized sexual morality' as harmful of Islamic society and nation. For him, the modernizing and secularizing reform of Pahlavi Shah was nothing but 'westoxification'—denial of freedom, dignity and equality to men and women and attempt to reduce the Iranian women as 'sexual object'. It is for this reason, in addition to others, that he vehemently opposed the White Revolution (1963) of the Shah that had conferred the right to vote to Iranian women. The opposition caused his exile to Iraq from where he guided the Iranian opposition to the Shah regime.

2.2 Khomeini, Women Question and White Revolution

This Islamic vision of Khomeini that interconnects the gender, polity and nation can be seen from the following statements which he issued from time to time. For instance, as early as in 1940s in opposition to westernizing policies of Pahlavi regime he stated that:

"Of course, they regard the civilization and advancement of the country as being dependent upon women's going naked in the streets, or to quote their own idiotic words, turning half the population into workers by unveiling them (we know only too well what kind of work is involved here). They will not agree to the country's being administered rationally and in accordance with God's law". [3]

He further states:

"The undertaking to remove the veil of modesty from the heads of virtuous Muslim women was spurred by carnal desires and is now rampant in the country at variance with religion and the laws, yet no one utters a word against it". [4]

In 1963 Khomeini opposed vehemently the Shah's White revolution and remarked:

"The entry of women into Parliament, Provincial and County Councils and Town Councils contravenes the indisputable laws of Islam, the interpretation of which, according to the text of the Constitution, is given over to the learned `ulama and the marja'e, no one else having the right to interfere. The jurists of Islam and the Muslims' marja'e have issued an edict forbidding it. Likewise the abrogation of the qualification that electors and candidates must be Muslim, which is stipulated in the said law, and replacing the policy of swearing the oath on the Holy Qur'an to one which stipulates swearing on a 'holy book', are an infringement of the said law, are dangerous for Islam and the independence of the country, and have been carried out either unintentionally or, God forbid, with malice aforethought". [5]

In the same year he further criticized the White Revolution as violation of *Qur'an*, *Shari'a* and Islamic law:

"The ruling regime (of the Shah) in Iran infringed upon the holy Islamic laws and is now set to violate the unequivocal and mandatory laws of the Qur'an. The honour and dignity of the Muslims are about to be violated and through legislation, which contravenes Shari'a, law and the Constitution, the tyrannical regime means to put chaste women to shame and humiliate the Iranian nation. The tyrannical regime intends to introduce legislation and implement equal rights for men and women, in other words it means to trample underfoot the incontrovertible and mandatory laws of Islam and the Most Noble Qur'an. They want to force 18-year-old girls to do military service and drag them to the barracks. At the point of the bayonet they mean to force young, chaste Muslim girls into centres of fornication". [6]

Later, in response to the passing of the Family Protection Law 1967 that granted legal rights to women for divorce and child custody, Khomeini announced "that women whose divorces had been decreed by the court against their husband's will would be committing adultery (*zena)* if they remarried". [7]

2.3 Islamic Revolution and Women's Participation

The 1979 Revolution was a turning point for Iranian women. It saw the massive participation of women from all walks of life-secular, religious, urban, rural, rich, poor, young, old- all participated and supported the revolution. Haideh Moghissi [8] has described the women who joined the revolution as belonging to three different social groups. The first of these groups included highly educated women of the new middle class with nationalist or socialist tendencies who supported the revolution and not the clerics. The reasons for their support were no different than their male counterparts—they sought the overthrow of the Shah and an end to foreign economic and political domination and, in the absence of an alternative, readily accepted Khomeini's leadership.

The second group comprised the marginalized urban lower-class women for whom the revolution provided a prospect for change in the material conditions of their lives. Moghissi refers to these women as having neither a coherent sense of themselves as distinct nor a particular affiliation with Islamic ideology. Rather, like the men in their lives, these women supported the clerical leaders who made specific economic promises such as lowering the prices of water and electricity as well as the more equitable distribution of oil revenues among the general population.

The third group of women participants were from the *bazaari* (mercantile) and traditional households. These women were the most resistant to and disturbed by the modernizing policies of the Shah. They had the least amount of education and identified most closely with conservative Islamic values and beliefs. This group was, and many still are, the most ardent supporters of the clerical leaders of the revolution. No matter their group affiliation however, these women were acting primarily as Iranians with the same basic complaints about the regime as their male counterparts. "*They too opposed the corruption and repression of the Pahlavi government and experienced the economic hardship which accompanied increasing inflation. Women were as horrified as men by the violent way in which peaceful demonstrations were dealt with by the government. They also suffered: women perished in the fire at the Rex movie theatre in Abadan attributed to the regime; they died in great numbers in Jaleh Square on Black Friday—September 8, 1978—alongside men*". [9]

Another peculiar development of the revolution concerned the issue of veiling. In the years since Reza Shah's abdication, forced unveiling (although technically still a law) was no longer strictly enforced, which meant the return of veiled women alongside secular non-veiled women on the streets of Iranian cities. However, during the revolutionary era, many secular middle-class women adopted the veil as a temporary action that symbolized their rejection of the regime and its "immoral" gender ideology. In time, wearing a traditional black *chador* (full body sheath) became the symbol of the popular revolution [10] and its denunciation of the Shah, rather than an overtly religious or Islamic statement. Nevertheless, adoption of these religious symbols and slogans did induce more and more women, particularly from the more traditional segments of society to join the demonstrations. [11]

Finally, the participation of women in the revolution was so decisive that members of the clerical community acknowledged and praised women as a critical component to the revolution's ultimate success. In fact, Ayatollah Khomeini, who in 1963 was the chief opponent to women's voting rights, publicly acknowledged women's social and political agency during the revolution: "*Women do more for [revolutionary] movement than men; their participation doubles that of men. That Muslim women are to be locked up in their homes is an utterly false idea that some attribute to Islam. Even during early Islam, women were active in the armies and war fronts*". [12] He promised the genuine freedom and equality to women which are clear from his following statements that were made during the course of Islamic revolution:

"*Islam put women on a par with men, and made them equal with men. Of course, there are certain Islamic precepts, which apply only to men, and others which apply only to women, but this does not mean that Islam discriminates between men and women*". [13]

He further stated in 1978 at the threshold of the Islamic revolution:

"*The Muslim women of Iran are currently participating in the political struggle and the demonstrations against the Shah. I have been told that in some Iranian cities they hold political meetings. In the Islamic system, women will have the same rights as men: the right to education, the right to work, the right to own property, the right to vote, the right to stand for election. In all aspects that men have rights, women have the same rights. However, there are some things unlawful for men, because of the corruption they create in men, and others unlawful for women because of their tendency to corrupt women. Islam wants the human dignity of both men and women to be safeguarded. It doesn't want women to be playthings in the hands of men. The image they have portrayed abroad of women being treated harshly under Islam is not a correct one"*. [14]

Notwithstanding women's active and publicly lauded participation and Imam Khomeini's public statement about the guaranteeing the equality and freedom during the revolution, they were soon targeted by the regime's rapid Islamization policies that led Nobel laureate Shirin Ebadi to remark in her memoir, Iran Awakening, highlighting the contradiction: "*That day, a feeling of pride washed over me that in hindsight makes me laugh. I felt that I too had won, alongside this victorious revolution. It took scarcely a month for me to realize that, in fact, I had willingly and enthusiastically participated in my own demise. I was a woman and this revolution's victory demanded my defeat*". [15]

2.4 Khomeini, Constitution and Women

Rapid Islamisation was one of the first strategies adopted by the Islamic regime to consolidate their political position. Ayatollah Khomeini's Islamisation policies got off the ground with gender relations as first and foremost target. The Islamisation of the family and sexual relation was prioritized which clearly demonstrated that the new political order had to be constructed around transformed gender relations. *Ayatollah Khomeini was adamant that without the Islamic family and women's hejab there could be no Islamic society. Women were the markers of the boundaries of the Islamic community and makers of Islamic identity.* [16]

On 26 February, nearly two weeks after the revolution of 1979, Khomeini's office announced that the Family Protection Law was to be abrogated. On 3 March, it was announced that the women would be barred from becoming judges. The next day Khomeini announced that initiating divorce would be an exclusively male prerogative. On 6 March, Ministry of Defence announced that women could no longer serve in the army. On 7 March, Khomeini said in a speech that women should wear *hejab* in the work places. On March 9, women were banned from participation in the sports, including the Olympic team. On 29 March, it was announced that the beaches would be segregated.

The Constitution of the Islamic Republic of Iran was adopted by referendum on October 24, 1979, and went into force on December 3 of the same year, replacing the Constitution of 1906. [17] The Constitution of the Islamic Republic of Iran was the formalized expression of the revolutionary transformation from modernization to Islamisation. It was a product of the aforementioned process of power struggle and political repression, and reflected the clash of ideas and balance of forces within the transitional period. [18] The Constitution established the legal principles of the new Islamist state, which involved rule by an appointed cleric known as the supreme leader (*Faqih*).

The constitution considered women and family as the main element in the identity of the Islamic nation. Women, as the link between family and Islamic society featured prominently in the Constitution's twelve chapters and 174 articles which set out to explain 'the political, social, cultural and economic institutions and relations there are to exist in our society and to establish an ideal and model society on the basis of Islamic criteria'. [19] The special status accorded to family and women as a part of 'imagined Islamic nation' is clearly reflected in the Preamble, Article 10 and 21 of the Constitution of Islamic Republic. Thus, whereas Preamble under the heading 'Women in the Constitution' highlights the importance of family and women in the Islamic vision of nation which states that, "*In the establishing of Islamic foundations human energies, which have been in the complete service of foreign exploitation, will regain their identity and human rights. In this regaining, it is natural that women, who have suffered greater oppression, up to now, from the tyrannical system, will enjoy more of a fulfilment of their rights.*

The family is the fundamental unit of society and the main centre of growth and transcendence for humanity. The concordance of ideals and ideology in the forming of a family as the main provider of the ground for the evolutionary movement and development of human beings is a basic principle and the providing of principles, and the provision of the possibility for achieving this purpose is one of the responsibilities of the Islamic government.

With such percepts, women, as a unit of society will no longer be regarded as a 'thing' or a tool serving consumerism and exploitation. In regaining her important duty and most respectful role of a mother in the nourishing of human beings devoted to their ideology, as an avant-gaurade with men, as a warrior in the active battlefields, of life the result will be her accepting a more serious responsibility and in the view of Islam, she will assume higher value and dignity". [20]

Article 10 of the Constitution enjoins and commands all relevant laws, rules and regulations to be at the service of the creation and sustenance of family: "*Considering that the family unity is the fundamental unit of Islamic society, all relevant laws, regulations and planning provisions should serve the purpose of facilitating the establishing of families and safe guarding the sacredness of the family institution and strengthening family relations on the basis of the Islamic Law and morality*". [21]

Further Article 21 binds the government to guarantee specified rights belonging to women: "*The government is obliged to guarantee women's rights according to Islamic criteria and provide the followings:*

1.# Favourable conditions for the fostering of the character of the women and restoration of her material and spiritual rights.

2.# Support of mothers, in particular, during pregnancy, and child care, and protection of children who are without guardian.

3.# Establishment of a competent court for the protection of the existence and stability of the family.

4.# Establishment of a special insurance for widows, elderly women and women without guardian

5.# Entrusting the guardianship of children to worthy mothers for the benefit of the children in cases where there is no legal guardian according to Islamic law". [22]

In addition to Article 10, 21 and provision of Preamble as stated above Article 3, 20, 28, 30, 32, 43, 151, and 163 lays down the broad framework for social welfare rights including education and employment which is also applicable women as these Articles are applicable for both sexes. However, what is clear from the analysis of these constitutional provisions and the policies and programmes that were implemented by the Islamic regime, which is detailed later in this chapter, that in the Constitution, women as citizens and political beings were subjugated to women as mothers. Since the women's role within the family was a special one, motherhood was considered higher in status with other dimensions of womanhood. The issue of how women's citizenship and political roles were dependent on her motherhood role is evident from the several works. [23]

2.5 Constitutional Implications of Articles for Women

The Constitution referred to Islamic law as extra constitutional criteria in many of its articles. This was particularly the case in relation to women especially in Articles 20, 21,151, and 163. As a consequence, the issue of women's constitutional rights was left to be debated and decided by the state agencies within the frame of undefined Islamic law and outside the boundaries of the constitution. Similarly, Article 20 stated that men and women should enjoy equal rights in conformity with Islamic criteria. The precise nature of equality of women with men in Islamic society was left vague and put in the hands of state to determine.

Similarly, Article 21, which was about protection of mothers and the family, also put the obligation of assuring the rights of women in all respects in conformity with Islamic criteria on the shoulders of the state. It avoided clarification on what the rights of women in conformity with Islamic criteria were. Article 151 qualified the requirement that the government should provide military training for all its citizens by stating that it should be done in conformity with Islamic criteria. It therefore left it unclear whether or not women had the right to participate in the military defence of the country. Article 163, which specified the attributes and qualifications of a judge, did not specify whether a person's gender was a qualification for becoming a judge was left to the unspecified opinion of the faith of the time.

The vagueness and inherent contradictions of the provision of Constitution vis-à-vis women allowed the Islamic regime to enunciate the policies and programs in order to construct its 'imagined Islamic nation'.

2.6 State Policies and Their Impact on Women

After the consolidation of state power by regime the state set out to implement the constitutional provisions relating to gender relations and actualize the ideal Islamic family proposed in it. Beneath this constitutional provision also lies an attempt to control women's sexuality. As Fatima Mernissi has noted that, "the sexual power attributed to women has caused the Islamic states to contain and control their sexuality through such social institutions such as the veil, the family, the marriage and divorce system and the legal system". [24] This was, however, set against the context of Islamic diversity, power struggles, political repression, ideological control, economic stagnation, war and destruction, and international isolation. The gender policy of the Islamic state was not a straight replica of the *Qur'an*, *Shari'a* or any other ready-made Islamic gender policy. The agenda of Islamisation of gender roles was gradually transformed into public policy that was most visible in the following fields:

2.6.1 Marriage: Given regime's thrust on 'family' as sacred institution the regulation of marriage assumes central importance in the Islamic scheme of Khomeini's regime: *Islam deals with the issue of your marriage even before you prepare to marry. Unlike the anarchic lifestyle of animals, Islam wants the fruit of your marriage to be a healthy human being. Before marriage, there are laws in Islam stipulating whom she should choose for a mate, whom he should choose as a wife. Characteristics of a man, characteristics of a woman, these are stipulated in Islam. In no other government can you find specifications about the man, about the woman, about the time of marriage, what kind of relationship should exist between the couple after they get married, what kind of life that should have.* [25] Thus, the state policy on marriage focused on the construction of marriage as the only legitimate site of sexual pleasure and reproduction, and its universalisation. To achieve this state adopted a number of strategies:

Firstly, the minimum age of marriage was lowered, which became nine for girls and fifteen for boys. Fathers or *vali's* (guardians) could arrange the marriage of a pre-pubescent girl to a much older man of his choice (Article 1041 of Civil Code). [26] In addition to the age condition, women had to obtain paternal consent for first marriage (Article 1044 of Civil Code). [27]

Secondly, another strategy for the universalisation of marriage was polygamy. The abolition of the Family Protection Law removed previously existing restrictions on polygamy which required a man to obtain permission from his first wife or from court before embarking on his second marriage. The removal of this restriction meant that a man could marry up to four permanent wives without any legal problems.

The Islamic regime's policy on marriage had adverse effects on women. A three year study of suicide amongst women, which was conducted in a Mashad hospital, concluded that 67 percent of women's suicides were caused by marriage problems. [28] In another survey, 75 percent of women who were divorcee said that their husbands use to regularly beat them. [29]

However the rising opposition to this state of affairs forced the regime to introduce some legal remedies for women. Some of the initial family rights that were granted to men were gradually watered down. The husband's right to prevent his wife from taking up employment was now limited. The High Council of the Judiciary ruled that if, "a woman worked before marriage or took a job with her husband's agreement after marriage, he could not lawfully prevent her from continuing to work. Even if a woman had started to work without her husband's permission, the ruling stated, he could only prevent her from working if he could prove that her job was contrary to the interest and reputation of the family". [30]

A new marriage contract was devised to help women in order to have some control over the kind of marriage they entered into. [31] The marriage contract spelled out those infringements of women's rights which could give them the right to initiate divorce. Some of the grounds upon which women can initiate divorce were: husband's refusal to pay *nafagheh*, husband's long-term illness or insanity, his employment in jobs demeaning to her and her family, husband's imprisonment for over five years, addiction, unreasonable absence from home for over six months, the husband's infertility or impotence and his marriage to another woman without her consent.

By 1985, the newspapers were already talking about 'the crisis of marriage'. The factors commonly listed as having contributed to the crisis of marriage included the housing shortage, decreasing incomes, unemployment and other economic problems. Rafsanjani complained that despite Islamic Republic's ideological receptivity to marriage, the age of marriage has in fact risen. The mean age of marriage increased within a similar range from 18.4 in 1966 to 19.7 in 1986. [32]

2.6.2 Divorce: Article 1133 of Civil Code grants men unilateral right to divorce: The husband may divorce his wife whenever he wishes to do so". [33] Ayatollah Khomeini instructed a woman could ask for divorce if her man was insane, impotent or infertile, absent from home without reason, imprisoned or unable to support the women. [34] These were also the reasons stated in the Civil Code. Under Article 1130, women may seek divorce under the conditions of '*usr va harj*', that is, if living with the husband is absolutely unbearable. [35] Also, *iddeh*, the waiting period was reinstated. Thus, a husband who chose to take his wife back within three months of unilateral divorce could simply do so, without considering her wishes and the state reinforced this.

This new law became the subject of protest and discussion, not only on the part of the secular women but also on Muslim reformist women. By early 1984, twelve conditions were inserted in the official marriage contract as grounds for the wife to acquire divorce, assuming the husband agreed to these conditions before the marriage ceremony. [36]

However court cases took longer on average for women if divorce case was initiated by women. [37] The courts expected women to back up their complaints with stronger evidence than they expected from men. Mrs. Behrouzi, *Majles* deputy complained that, "some special civil courts expect woman to bear all the problems and submit to their husband whims under all circumstances". [38] In many cases, women were divorced without their knowledge and in their absence. There is ample evidence that in many cases wife's agreement was secured by intimidation and threat of violence. [39]

To avoid paying maintenance, men often abused their wives to make them leave their homes; and petitioned the courts that their wives were disobedient (*adam-e tamkin*). Even in such cases courts often advised women to go back to their home and try patch things up with their husbands. [40] These complaints prompted initiation of a campaign in the first decade of IRI for curtailment of male divorce rights. Thus, in 1989, the government reintroduced a clause of the abolished Family Protection Law according to which all divorces had to have court permission before being registered in notary public offices.

2.6.3 Family Planning: Population control and family planning were condemned as an imperialist conspiracy to violate the rights of the Islamic nation and impair its growth and prosperity. Although contraceptives were not banned, supplies became erratic and prices skyrocketed. Ayatollah Khomeini emphasized that women's control of their fertility without their husband's permission was against Islam. Rafsanjani further added that, birth control was against women's Islamic duty to bear children and that in Islam "*women do not have a right to avoid pregnancy and feeding of their infants*". [41]

Couples with seven or more children received a plot of land on which to build a home. Reports stated that middle-class couples tended to have larger families in the 1980s than they used to have in the 1970s. [42] It has also been observed, 'that many women, who decided two children were enough for them prior to the revolution, had a 'second set of children' after the revolution. Having a larger family was, thus, intended to reduce the likelihoods of their husbands taking on additional financial responsibilities. In this manner, women hoped that even if they did lose their husbands, at least they would not be robbed of their children'. [43] Consequently, the overall, fertility rates increased from 6.3 to 7.0 in 1986, as Iran's population expanded and reached to 50 million, according to the 1986 census. [44] By 1989, the population reached 55 million with an annual rate of increase of 3.2 percent. [45]

However the chronically ill economy, the devastation of national resources as a result of war against Iraq, high unemployment and the housing crisis, all contributed to the Islamic state's awakening to the political consequences of rapid population growth under the existing circumstances.

The process of reversal policy began in 1988 through the state's initiation of public debate on the issue of population control. In July 1989, Dr. Malekafzali, Deputy Minister of Health, announced the government's policy on population control. He explained that, 'the policy would be based on distribution of free contraceptives through the newly set up health centres in rural and urban areas which would cover 90 percent of the population. The contraceptives, including IUD, pills and condoms, had been imported from Western countries, he announced. Asked about the forms of birth control, he emphasized that government policy was in line with Ayatollah Khomeini's instructions that abortion, regardless of the stage of pregnancy and sterilization were prohibited in Islam. He also reaffirmed the state's support of the husband's control over his wife's fertility by emphasizing that women should not use birth control without their husband's agreement.' [46] The state also requested assistance from the UN fund for population activities.

2.6.4 Bride Price: *Mehrieh*, as bride price, was normally specified in the marriage contract and was payable to the woman by the man after consummation of marriage .But traditionally woman's mehrieh was paid by the man upon divorce. Article 1086 of the Civil Code stated that *mehrieh* would not be paid to a woman if she refused to submit herself sexually to her husband. [47] Article 1088 stated that if the husband died before consummation of marriage, the wife would not be entitled to *mehrieh.* [48] Article 1092 granted the woman half of her *mehrieh* if she was divorced by her husband before consummation. [49] In addition to above it needs to emphasize here that state assistance to women in securing payment of *mehrieh* remained rhetorical when it came to enforcement.

2.6.5 Inheritance: As per the conventional Islamic rule women inherits half of what men did. Moreover, women could not inherit land and were only entitled to a share from the sale of property and not the property itself (Articles 946 and 947 of Civil Code). A man inherits his entire wife's wealth, but she is entitled to one-fourth (if he has no child) or one-eighth (if he has children). This is only in case of permanent marriage; partners in temporary marriage receive no inheritance. In polygamous marriages, wives must decide amongst themselves the allotted inheritance, which according to 942 of the Civil Code can never exceed their designated fourth or eighth.

2.6.6 Child Custody: According to 1169 of the Civil Code, on divorce, the mother shall have the custody of her son until the age of two and of her daughter until the age of seven. Unless, of course, she forfeits custody prior to these dates due to remarriage or insanity. From the child's birth, the father has legal guardianship and obtains custody when the mother's term expires. In the absence of the father, the paternal grandfather receives guardianship. The same was reinforced in many of the court decisions. In the closing years of the first decade of the Islamic Republic political pressures was still directed towards a redefinition of custody without much success.

2.6.7 *Hejab:* The process of the imposition of hejab was a long and difficult one and it became one of the most fiercely implemented policies of the Islamic Republic. By the summer of 1980, instructions were issued to the public sector warning employees that they should either enforce *hejab* on their women employees or sack them. [50] A large numbers of women were sacked for not complying with *hejab-e-eslami* (Islamic Dress). [51] This was followed by the official definition of women given by the Council of the Revolution as 'covering of the head and all of the body except for the circle of the face and hands from the wrist'. [52]

The next step was to extend the imposition of *hejab* to female users of public services. Women not wearing *hejab* were refused entry to public premises; they were also banned from travelling with the national airline without *hejab*. [53] Shops were ordered to refuse to sell goods to women not wearing Islamic Dress. [54] The private sector was the next target and private offices and factories were instructed by the state to observe the Islamic *hejab* code for their female employees. Women's *hejab* became legally compulsory in 1983 when the *Majles* passed the Islamic punishment law (Flogging). This law specified seventy four lashes as punishment for the lack of strict observance of law. [55] No women dared to appear in public without Islamic dress because so many women bones were broken and faces burned with acids. [56]

2.6.8 Alimony: Similar problems, operated in relation to woman's *nafagheh* (alimony is payable after divorce to a woman if she has child custody) which according to *Shari'a* was payable under two circumstances. First, during *iddeh*, or the waiting period. Second, *nafagheh* was also payable to the wife if she was in lawful custody of children from the marriage. In both the cases, *nafagheh*, could be withdrawn if divorce was due to the woman's immorality or refusal to have sex with her husband. [57] Women who were over child bearing age and did not have to observe the waiting period did not receive anything.

Like other family related issue, the question of *nafagheh* for divorced women became the subject of intense lobbying by the Islamic women's movement. The campaign culminated in the number of Majles proposals. But despite its frequent revival the idea of marriage compensation did not become law in the first decade of the Islamic Republic.

2.7 The Law of Retribution

The Retribution Law (*Ghanun Ghesas*) was passed by the Majles in 1982. An analysis of 199 articles of the retribution law demonstrates the inherent bias in these laws against women. For instance, the body of a woman was worth half that of a man as reflected in the clauses dealing with murder (Articles 5, 6, 46). [58] Similarly if a Muslim man wilfully murders a Muslim woman he will be sentenced to *ghesas* but the woman's guardianship must pay the murderer one half of his blood money before he receives *ghesas* (Article 5). However Article 6: If a Muslim woman wilfully murders a Muslim man, she will be sentenced only to *ghesas* and will not be entitled to *diyeh* or blood money (Article 6). Second, the judgment of a woman was valued as half that of a man as reflected in the clauses dealing with testimony (Articles 33, 91,128,167). [59] Third, woman's reproductive function took priority over her life (Articles 50, 90, 103,104). [60]

The retribution law created horrifying atmosphere of violence and revenge which claimed many female victims. By 1983 it was reported, at least hundred acts of retribution had already taken place in IRI. [61]

The rate of domestic violence was reported to be as high as 72 percent. [62] Many incidents of domestic violence ended with a woman's death or serious injury. [63] A report on the work of the Penal Courts in Mashad indicated that damages paid by women to men for causing injury was more than double the amount due to the woman if a man caused the injury. [64] Newspaper accounts of domestic violence also demonstrated the extent to which men were taking the law into their hands to decide and administer Islamic justice on women. A twenty eight year old woman was knifed thirty-five times by a group of men who were her brothers and cousins. They confessed to having killed her because she kept leaving the house without permission and eventually when he saw her with a strange man, so they decided to kill her. [65]

The second aspect of the Islamisation of women's position concerned women's participation in national development. The Islamic Republic formulated a series of policies on women's social participation, including in education, employment and politics.

2.8 Women's Education

Contrary to expectations by secular forces, the Islamic state did not prevent women from engaging in education. Indeed, women's education was considered as an important strategy for the Islamisation of society. The women, as the link between family and nation, had to participate in both the processes: as a mother for the child and as a teacher for the pupil. Furthermore, women's presence in educational institutions was a political urgency. The Islamic state had to fill the schools and universities with its female supporters to counteract the influence of the secular middle classes.

Islamisation of educational system was achieved through

more religious instructions, mandatory teaching of Arabic in secondary schools, dropping of English at primary level and the teaching of a heavily biased history of Islam and Islamic revolution, gender segregation in the education system, imposition of *hejab* on women, reinforcement of gender division of subjects, and preservation of male dominance in education. The policy of segregation in the education system started in March 1979 with banning of the mixed classes in private educational institutions and later by attempts to segregate classes in universities and polytechnics. The gender division of subjects was reflected in the introduction of new courses in 1982 that was limited to following subjects in girl's high schools: first year, knitting and needle work, second year, sewing, third year hygiene, safety and first aid, and fourth year, nutrition and child care. [66]

In general, with regard to female literacy and schooling the census of 1986 indicated that the rate of literacy amongst the urban women had risen from 55.1 percent in 1976 to 65.2 percent in 1986. Literacy amongst rural women was standing at 36 percent as compared to 16.5 percent in 1976. [67] This was due to the fact that the Islamic Republic reintroduced segregation and veiling and increased the religious content of the curriculum, emphasizing traditional culture. Thus, while cultivating their own vision of society and ideology, the regime made educational institutions more acceptable to the traditional classes. Ideologically, the regime benefited from promoting this form of education and indeed, many conservatives considered the introduction of Islamic education the frontline against cultural imperialism and Westernization. Therefore, promotion of female literacy served the regime's purposes and helped them to refute the claim that the *ulema* were against women's education.

With regard to women's higher education, the policy adopted by the Islamic Republic proved contradictory and controversial, and as a result had to be amended a number of times. It may be noted that before the Revolution, women were entitled to pursue their studies in all fields of knowledge except mining. However, after the Revolution, women's entry into the educational field was severely curtailed, particularly in the field of technical, engineering and experimental sciences. Women were denied admission in many fields like engineering, agriculture, aviation, political science, law, management and even veterinary medicine etc. [68] Moreover, restrictions were imposed on women's admission to most medical, environmental and human sciences by specifying a maximum number of places for women which ranged from 20 to 50 percent. Women who were attending the prohibited courses were asked to either drop out or change subject. On the whole, slightly over half of all subjects offered within higher education were closed to women. [69]

Training for favoured professions, such as teaching, nursing and midwifery, was encouraged at all levels from schools to university. The most rapidly expanding area of women's education was Islamic theology. For women to be eligible for government scholarship to study abroad, she must be married and accompanied by her husband.

The number of women in university education remained steady from mid-1970s.Women constituted 28.5 percent of the university students in 1974-75 and 29.9 percent in 85-86. [70] However, the pattern of female distribution in various subjects changed. The statistical trend in the first decade of the Islamic Republic indicated a small rise from 37 percent in 1979 to 38.5 percent in 1987, in the number of female students in social sciences and humanities combined; another small rise from 40 to 41 percent in the same year in educational sciences; and a more substantial rise from 33 to 38 percent in natural and mathematical sciences. Again in the same year a substantial drop out occurred from 21 to 10 percent in agricultural subjects; from 9 to 4 percent in engineering; and from 54 to 45 percent in medicine and Para medical subjects. [71] With regard to education broad only 13.5 percent of students abroad were women. [72]

In May 1989, restrictions on women's entry to geology and agriculture were lifted. Women's entry quotas in various fields were abolished altogether in medical, para-medical and some engineering fields and were increased in some technical and industrial subjects. This was the result of lobbying by women's social and the cultural council and reflected the unpredictable nature of the IRI's policies on women. Women's council appealed to President Khamenei and the reluctant Planning Committee, which took final decisions on higher education agreed to some concessions. This change of policy demonstrated that changes in IRI's policies depended on the good will of the leaders and far from being rooted in Islam, they were conjunctural. [73]

2.9 Women's Employment

No other aspect of women's social involvement, however, presented such problems for the Islamic Republic's policy-makers as did women's employment. The early post-revolutionary years witnessed a number of attacks on women's employment. Women were barred from becoming judges immediately after the revolution. Women were barred from singing and or giving recreational programmes on radio and television. The age of retirement for women was reduced from 50 to 45 years and their years of service were reduced from 30 to 25 to make them eligible for retirement. [74]

Compensation packages were enacted that allowed women to retire after only 15 years of employment. Day-care centres were closed down and women were given the option of transferring their full salaries to their husbands or working part-time in order to devote themselves more fully to their husbands. [75] Women were also restricted from certain professions and directed into other sectors seen as more in-line with their domestic and motherhood responsibilities such as nursing and teaching. The next step was to cleanse the workplace and the first and foremost target was the public sector where the intelligentsia of the Pahlavi era had spread roots.

However, once the transitional period was over and the Islamic regime felt politically secure, the emphasis of the state policy began to change from an ad hoc replacement of Pahlavi practices to that of formulating a more systematic policy on women's employment. The main elements of the new policy included an emphasis on the ideological importance of training women for certain professions such as education, welfare, health and medicine, and the adaptation of women's employment to the needs of the 'Islamic family'. The first legislation in this respect was the draft proposal on midwifery training and to build more midwifery training centres and training of 20,000 midwives. [76]

At the policy level, the IRI acknowledged the value of women's work outside the home, yet it adapted women's employment to meet the needs of the family. Women's employment was directed to those professions which were seen to be compatible with women's nature and her family responsibilities.

As a result the participation of women in workforce remained very low. Official statistics showed a decline in women's economic activity from 12.9 percent in 1976 to 8.1 percent in 1986. A very tiny proportion of women worked in occupations of specialist nature, i.e.0.26 percent, 13.4 percent worked in production and transport, 8.6 percent in administration and 5.3 percent in services. [77] Women's representation was largest in female occupations such as teaching and nursing. There was a sharp decline in the proportion of women factory workers, from 20 percent in 1976 to 7 in 1983. [78]

However under pressure from women organizations the government introduced legislation, passed by the *Majles* in 1983 and modified in late 1985, making half time employment in government services formally open to women and eligible for certain benefits. [79] Contrary to the initial assault against day care centres as an imperialist ploy to separate mother from children, in 1988, the office of the Prime Minister issued an instruction to all ministries and government organizations to set up work place nurseries. [80] The labour Laws were amended in 1987 to include clauses related to women's health and safety. Article 75 prohibited the carrying of heavy weights and undertaking dangerous work for women workers. Article 76 prohibited night shifts except in education, health and medical work. Article 77, maternity leave was provided with 90 days, half of which should be taken after child birth. Breast feeding mothers were granted half an hour leave every three hours to feed their babies (Article 79). [81]

The Islamic state did not ban women's employment outside the home. But the state was more interested in imposing a particular gender division of labour at work rather than pushing women out of the labour force altogether.

2.10 Political Process

After the revolution, various factions of the state and revolutionary grass-roots organizations attempted to harness women's tremendous mobilization potential. The state took control of women's mass mobilization by organizing mass rallies in support of the state's Islamisation policies and against the demands of both secular and Islamic opposition. Prior to each election, an extensive campaign was launched to encourage people to vote. Magazines published articles which described the women's vote as a 'national, political and Islamic duty'. [82]

Women's participation in the Iran-Iraq war was also encouraged by the state. Ayatollah Khomeini made several rousing speeches to promote women's strategic importance. Women were recruited as revolutionary guards and mobilized for military action. Despite his earlier statement that Islam does not allow women's participation in a holy war *(Jihad),* Ayatollah Khomeini instructed women to take up military training in the name of Islam to defend their country. [83]

Despite their relative success in pressurizing for improvements in Islamic rights for women, Islamic women leaders were on the whole presented with limited opportunity to enter into top decision-making, and struggled to find a role for themselves in the higher echelons of the Islamic society. Eleven elections during the first decade of the Islamic Republic produced 6 women *Majles* representatives in all. This was even more tokenistic than in the Shah's regime, where in the last Pahlavi Majles and Senate, out of 270 members only 18 were women and only one woman was a Minister. [84]

Endnotes

1. Shahidian, Hammed (2002), "Gender Politics in Islamic Republic", p. 164, Greenwood Press, London.
2. Ibid.
3. The position of women from the viewpoint of Imam Khomeini *(May Allah Grant him Peace).* The institute of Compilation and Publication of Imam Khomeini's Works (International Affairs Division). Translated by Juliana Shah and Behrooz Arezoo, Autumn 2001, Tehran, Islamic Republic of Iran, p. 126, available at: http://www.iranchamber.com/history/rkhomeini/books/women_position_khomeini.pdf.
4. Ibid., p. 132.
5. Ibid., p. 134.
6. Ibid., p. 138.
7. Hoodfar, Homa (1999), "The Women's Movement in Iran: Women at the Crossroads of Secularization and Islamicization", p. 20, available at: http://connection.ebscohost.com/c/articles/2436875/womens-movement-iran-women-crossroads-secularization-islamization.
8. Moghissi, Haideh (1991), "Women, Modernization and Revolution in Iran", *Review of Radical Political Economics*, Vol. 23, No. 3-4, pp. 206-208.
9. Betteridge, Anne H. (1983), "To Veil or Not to Veil: A Matter of Protest or Policy", in 'Women and Revolution in Iran' (ed), p. 114, Boulder: Westview Press.
10. Hoodfar, No. 7, p. 22.
11. Ibid.
12. Asef Bayat (2007), "A Women's Non-Movement: What It Means to Be a Woman Activist in an Islamic State", p. 172, *Comparative Studies of South Asia, Africa and the Middle East,*

27, No. 1.
13. The position of women from the viewpoint of Imam Khomeini, No. 3, p. 35.
14. Ibid.
15. Ebadi, Shirin (2006), "Iran Awakening: A Memoir of Revolution and Hope", p. 38, New York: Random House.
16. Paider, Parvin (1995), "Women and the Political Process in Twentieth Century Iran", p. 232, Cambridge: Cambridge University Press.
17. Ibid., p. 227.
18. Ibid., p. 227.
19. Algar, Hamid (translated) (1980), "Constitution of Islamic Republic", p. 19, Berkeley: Mizan Press.
20. Paidar, No. 16, p. 260.
21. Ibid.
22. Ibid., p. 261.
23. Paider, No.16, p. 260; Shahidian, No. 1, p. 114.
24. Mernissi, Fatima (1975), "Beyond the Veil: Male-Female Dynamics in a Modern Muslim Society", pp. xv, Bloomington: Indiana University Press.
25. The position of women from the viewpoint of Imam Khomeini, No. 3, p. 162.
26. Afary, Janet (2009), "Sexual Politics in Iran", p. 281, Cambridge University Press.
27. Ibid., p. 281.
28. Zan-e-Ruz, 4.6.89/13.3.68, quoted in Paider, No. 16, p. 283.
29. Keyhan, 16.7.88/25.5.67, quoted in Paidar, No. 16, p. 283.
30. Ghorbani, Farajollah, (1989), "Khanevadeh: Majmueh Kamel Ghavanin Va Mogharat (Family: The Complete Collection of Laws and Regulations)", quoted in Paider, No. 16, p. 284.
31. Iran Times, 13.6.86, quoted in Paider, No. 16, p. 284.
32. Statistical Centre of Iran (SCI), 1988c, p. 62, 1990, p. 12, quoted in Paider, No. 16, p. 284.
33. Shahidian, No. 1, p. 224.
34. Paider, No. 16, p. 290.
35. Shahidian, No. 1, p. 224.
36. Najmabadi, Afsaneh, (1994), "Power, Morality and the New Muslim Womanhood", in Weiner, Myron and Banuazizi, Ali (eds.), 'The Politics of Social Transformation in Afghanistan, Iran and Pakistan', 377, Syracuse University Press.

37. Ettelat, 23.10.85/31.6.64, quoted in Paider, No. 16, p. 292.
38. Ettelat,13.2.82/24.11.60, quoted in Paider, No. 16, p. 292.
39. Paider, No. 16, p. 292.
40. Afary, No. 26, p. 284.
41. Ettelat, 5.4.86/15.2.65, quoted in Paider, No.16, p. 287.
42. Hoodfar, Homa, (1996), "Bargaining with Fundamentalism: Women and the Politics of Population Control in Iran", 'Reproductive Health Matters, Fundamentalism, Women's Empowerment and Reproductive Rights", Vol. 4, No. 8, p. 36.
43. Ibid., p. 37.
44. Ibid., p. 32.
45. Keyhan (London), 2.7.89/11.4.68, quoted in Paider, No. 16, p. 288.
46. Ibid., pp. 288-289.
47. Ghorbani, Farajollah, (1989), "Khanevadeh: Majmueh Kamel Ghavanin Va Mogharat (Family: The Complete Collection of Laws and Regulations)", quoted in Paider, No. 16, p. 300.
48. Ibid.
49. Mohaqeq-Damad, Seyyed Mostafa (1986), "Barassi Feqhi Hoghugh Khanwvadeh: Nekah Va Enelal (A Jurisprudent Assessment of Family Rights), quoted in Paider, No. 16, p. 300.
50. Ettelaat, 6.7.80/15.4.59, quoted in Paider, No. 16, p. 338.
51. Poya, Maryam (1999), "Women, Work and Islamism: Ideology and Resistance in Iran", p. 66, Zed Books: London.
52. Bambad, 8.7.80/15.4.59, quoted in Paider, No.16, p. 338.
53. Ettelaat, 8.9.81/17.6.60, quoted in Paider, No. 16, p. 339.
54. Poya, Maryam, No. 51, p. 73.
55. Keyhan, 9.9.83/18.6.62, quoted in Paider, No. 16, p. 342.
56. Poya, Maryam, No. 51, p. 73.
57. Mohaqeq-Damad, Seyyed Mostafa (1986), "Barassi Feqhi Hoghugh Khanwvadeh: Nekah Va Enelal (A Jurisprudent Assessment of Family Rights), Tehran: Nashr Olum Eslami, 1365, quoted in Paider, No. 16, p. 300.
58. Tabari, A. and Yeganeh, N. (eds) (1982), "In the Shadow of Islam: The Women's Movement in Iran", p. 94, Zed Press, London.
59. Ibid., pp. 94-97.
60. Ibid.
61. Iranshahr, 12.8.83/21.5.62, quoted in Paider, No. 16, p. 352.
62. Keyhan (London), 7.9.85/18.11.64, quoted in Paider, No. 16, p.

352.
63. Keyhan (London), 7.9.85/18.11.64, quoted in Paider, No. 16, p. 352.
64. Keyhan (London), 7.9.85/18.11.64, quoted in Paider, No. 16, p. 352.
65. Ettelaat, 12.6.89/22.3.5, quoted in Paider, No. 16, p. 352.
66. Najmabadi, No. 36, p. 379.
67. Statistical Centre of Iran (1985) C.P. 12, 25, quoted in Paider, No. 16, p. 284.
68. Afary, No. 26, p. 305.
69. Mojab, Shahrzad (1991), "State Control and Women's Resistance in Iranian Universities", quoted in Paider, No. 16, p. 319.
70. Statistical Centre of Iran (1989), p. 15, quoted in Paider, No. 16, p. 320.
71. Paider, No. 16, p. 319.
72. Statistical Centre of Iran (1985), p. 35, quoted in Paider, No. 16, p. 320.
73. Paider, No. 16, p. 321.
74. Poya, No. 51, p. 67.
75. Esfandiari, Haleh (1997), "Reconstructed Lives: Women and Iran's Islamic Revolution", pp. 41-42, Washington DC: The Woodrow Wilson Centre Press.
76. Paider, No. 16, p. 350.
77. Statistical Centre of Iran (1988b), p. 9, quoted in Paider, No. 16, p. 335.
78. Moghadham, Valentine (1988), "Women, Work and Ideology in the Islamic Republic", *International Journal of Middle Eastern Studies,* Vol. 20, No. 2, p. 237.
79. Najmabadi, No. 36, p. 380.
80. Zan-e-Ruz, 17.7.88/26.5.67, quoted in Paider, No. 16, p. 329.
81. Ettellat, 24.10.87/2.8.66, quoted in Paider, No. 16, p. 327.
82. Yeganeh, Nahid (1993), "Women, Nationalism and Islam in Contemporary Political Discourse in Iran", *Feminist Review*, No. 44, p. 14.
83. Ibid.
84. Ibid.

3

Islam, State, Gender Discourse and Policies: Rafsanjani and Khatami Periods (1989-2005)

The death of Ayatollah Khomeini in June 1989 created a serious political vacuum in the Islamic Republic of Iran. The absence of Imam Khomeini, who had hitherto maintained a balance among the different power factions within the country's dispersed political system on account of his charisma, gave fillip to the rise of factionalism 'to the extent that ideological discord became one of the most prominent features of Iranian politics'. [1] On the other a decade long war with Iraq had left the country economically ruined at the end of the war in 1988, which in turn also increased the factional feud within the Iranian polity. These factional divisions played and continue to play an important role in shaping women's agenda and activism. Women—whether belonging to secular or Islamist viewpoints—subscribed to these various political and factional divides and use their political alliances to advance their gender agenda. This factional divide affects the state policies towards women.

3.1 Rafsanjani Period

It was under the above political context that Ali Akbar Hashemi Rafsanjani was elected to the office of presidency in 1989 on the reformist agenda. Earlier following the death of Imam Khomeini constitutional amendment was carried out which among others abolished the post of Prime Minister and transfer much of its power to the President and also clipped the power of *velayat-i-Faqih.* A weak *velayat-i-Faqih* along with powerful Presidency allowed Rafsanjani to pursue his policies without much constrain and implement his relatively liberal vision within the limit of constitutional structure of Islamic Republic of Iran during his two terms Presidency (1989-

1997). The period has been hailed as "Second Republic" on account of relatively liberal economic, political and cultural policies of Rafsanjani.

His primary focus was to end Iran's 'international isolation' and rebuild the sanction-afflicted and war-torn country. Accordingly he moved from politics of 'anti-West ideological rhetoric', characteristics of previous regime, and sought to attract the foreign investment by pursuing a relatively liberalized political, economic and socio-cultural programme, which also included the gender reform. This political positioning of President Rafsanjani was interlinked, in addition to his personal world view, to attract outside investment, particularly from the West. Rafsanjani's gender policies follow from this holistic policy and programme. Therefore, an analysis of his gender policies requires a brief outline of his economic, political and cultural policies and its impact on Iranian society.

He recognized the dire need for economic investment to rejuvenate Iran's ailing industries and weak economy after eight years of war. New economic and social policies were implemented to reconstruct the devastated infrastructures and to reorganize the economy. Rafsanjani attempted to introduce privatization and liberalizing economic policies to Iran's statist economic system despite the oppositions from conservatives and statists. The Gulf War of 1991 and the American destruction of Iraq's economy pushed oil prices up, and Iran benefited. The increase in oil revenue for Iran meant an increased GDP—according to UNDP an average annual growth rate of 2.4 percent between 1990 and 2003. [2]

As Iran gradually emerged from its international isolation and embarked on greater interactions with its outside world, many Iranian exiles returned home. Newspaper editorials and articles covered television and radio, however, remained firmly under state control. Emerging from years of fear and violence, the deprivation and oppression of a protracted war, and the punitive and puritanical policies of the state, the public found opportunities to demand accountability and ask for restoration of individual autonomy, civil liberties, human rights, women rights, and the like. Amidst this vacillating environment, marginalized intellectuals, religious leaders and members of the elite took advantage of the more open atmosphere to re-examine the political, social and economic status quo.

3.1.1 Gender Policy: Well before his accession to the presidency in 1989, Ali Akbar Hashemi Rafsanjani was promoting reform measures to improve the status of women. All of these reforms were rationalized largely in terms of Islamic norms. As a Speaker of *Majles* [Iranian Parliament] he encouraged women to participate in Iranian economy while retaining the 'Islamic morality'. He lauded the 'progressive' Islamic code of ethics that sanctions the full social participation of women. Earlier in 1988, as Chairman of the High Council of Cultural Revolution, he established the Social and Cultural Council of Women to promote women's economic and social activity. In 1992 the Office of Women's Affairs, an offshoot of the Presidential Bureau, was created to identify specific women related problems and shortcomings and to propose solutions to uplift social, political and economic status and role of women in the Iranian society. His priority to gender reform was evident from The First Economic, Social, Cultural Development Plan of the Islamic Republic (1989-93) that addressed female education and stated the following goals: [3]

1. Improving the condition of women through education and increasing women's participation in the socio-economic affairs of society and family.
2. Bringing about a higher level of participation among women in social, cultural, educational and economic affairs, while maintaining the values of the family and the character of Muslim women.

3.1.2 Women's Education: As discussed in the earlier chapter how initially the state has closed off subjects of study considered inappropriate for women including those in the technical, engineering and experimental sciences. In addition, quotas were also placed on female admission to medical, environmental and human sciences. Married women were also prevented from studying abroad without the presence of their husband. Gender stereotyping was evident in all school textbooks where the role of women, motherhood and *hejab* was enforced. Hence after coming to power in 1989, *Rafsanjani avowed that in "Islam, there are no barriers to the education of women in any field".* [4]

The government began to remove earlier policies that closed geology and agricultural programmes to women. Then the medical and engineering quotas were removed. By 1994, all barriers to specific fields of study were lifted for women [5] and as a result the number of female students increased in many fields of study. For example, in medicinal disciplines the number increased to 60 per cent. [6] In 1992, 42 percent of Iran's university graduates and roughly one-third of those with doctorates were women. [7]

3.1.3 Women's Employment: During the Iran–Iraq war millions of women worked as volunteers to help build the country's economy and win the war against Iraq which brought them into the public arena. Once the war was over, women could not be easily sent back home. It was revealed that Iran suffered from a dire shortage of professionals, many of whom had emigrated during the war. Recognizing the objective necessity of labour force President Rafsanjani admitted in 1990 that *"We are in need of a women's labour force" and encouraged women to play a larger role in Iranian arts, sports, politics, and religion".* [8]

Ayatollah Mohammad Yazdi also stated that in Islam "women enjoy the same rights as men". [9] The government policies along with support of a section of *ulema* led to a steady increase in women's economic activity, both in formal and informal sector. However, most of the women in Iran were employed in the state sector. Thus contrary to 1986, the proportion of active women to the total female population had dropped sharply from 10.8 percent in 1976-77 to 6.1 percent; it increased to 8.7 percent in 1991. [10] According to another estimate, women's participation in the labour force has tripled since 1986 to attain 18 percent in 1993. [11]

In addition to the increased importance of the Islamic professionals, the implementation of reconstruction policies also resulted in the return of secular middle class women professionals, particularly teachers and nurses, who had either voluntary left or had been dismissed from their posts during the revolutionary period. [12] A huge need for teachers, especially at the primary level, produced a great demand for women. [13] In fact the Islamic Republic’s idea of sexual segregation actually led to the expansion of certain jobs for women such as paediatricians and gynaecologists, while men have been discouraged from these medical specialties. Furthermore, with the opening of the economy and the increase in the relative size of the private sector, the demand for administrative jobs has increased and many women have found employment in the private sector, particularly in the expanding service sector.

In addition to education and health related profession, another sector where women made inroads was the legal arena. Thus in 1992, a law allowed women to sit as assistant judges in courts hearing divorce cases. A limited number of women started working as prosecutors and investigative judges who prepared cases for judges in court, but were barred from issuing judgements. To this extent the Rafsanjani government not only appointed 200 women judicial counsellors in 1996 in order to ensure more satisfactorily women's rights in courts but also encouraged to organize seminars and conferences on the subject matter of role of women in judiciary.

Thus a conference was organized in September 1996 to discuss the works of Ayatollah Muqadas-Ardibili who issued a fatwa authorizing women to become judges. Following this conference, Ayatollah Muhammad Yazdi, the head of the judiciary, declared that the question of the possibility for women to reoccupy this post is under study. As a result, for the first time in the Islamic Republic, a woman was appointed the vice director general of Tehran's justice department. Likewise, a woman was appointed a vice minister of public health. [14]

In addition to government policies and favourable political climate that helped women to play a larger role in the restructuring of the Iranian economy, the pressure for recognition of women's work as well as their greater demand also came from below. Thus many young, often educated women who had followed the Ayatollah and volunteered to marry handicapped war veterans (and provide them with full time nursing care) pressed for recognition of their unpaid work. These volunteer women who had given so much support to the Islamic regime slowly grow reluctant to continue their services for free while their male counterparts were paid. They demanded, and sometimes forced their way into paid positions. As a result, Islamic institutions that had been created during the early part of the revolution such as *Jihad sasandegi* increasingly started employing those who were either from the families of veterans of the war and revolution or had served as volunteers. [15]

Despite regime's push to integrate women in the work force, their fuller participation was constrained and limited on account of regime's identification of family as the prime responsibility of women. In his speech on Iran's women's day in 1991, President Rafsanjani stressed the, '*need for a law for part-time work allowing women to spend half their time in economic activities and the other half performing their domestic duties*'. [16] On the same day Ayatollah Khamenei, also reminded women that family was a natural institution and was the basis for women's activities, "*women with all their expertise and knowledge must first fulfil their family role*". [17] Thus, notwithstanding the law on providing the facility of nursery and right to breastfeed the babies during working hours, a number of women could not go out and work, principally due to high rate of nursery fees. [18]

Though the government provided paid maternity leave but

it was too short; most women took one or two years leave until the children were old enough to be left with their female kin. This put women at a disadvantage position in the labour market and had a negative effect on their grade, salary, years' of service, insurance and pension. [19] Further the provision of taking permission of husband or another male member for working outside put constraints on the freedom and mobility of women in seek employment, though in majority of the cases women got permission as women's earnings were essential for family's survival. [20]

Another major issue faced by women was the refusal to recognize women as breadwinners. Their benefits were calculated for a single person. A single person received half of a married person's allowances and subsidies. Women with children did not receive child benefit. Married women did not receive the married person's allowances. This reduced their salary drastically in comparison to men. For same reason women's tax, pension and retirement deductions allowances were calculated as for a single person.

After her death a woman's pension would stop while a man's pension would be transferred to his family. Women and men were entitled to health schemes but women could use the scheme only for themselves not for their families. In 1990, *Zan-e-Ruz* published an article describing the government's approval of the New Year bonus to workers. This also revealed the great differential treatment within the labour force and labour market. Each employee who is married and has children will receive 100,000 Rials. Each employee who is not married will receive 70,000 Rials. Married women are considered as single persons. [21]

Zanan, a monthly magazine reported in November 1990 that within the state sector 18 percent of women had higher education compared with only 6 percent of men. But only 3 per cent of these women occupied higher positions. [22] It was stated that, "In the eyes of law men and women may be equal but the employers treat men and women differently". [23]

3.1.4 Family Planning: One of the most successful public policy and programme of Rafsanjani government was an effective family planning. The 1986 national census estimated revealed a population growth of about 15 million since 1979. By 1990 the population had reached 59.5 million growing at an average rate of 3.9 percent. [24] Responding to the economic, social and political effects of this demographic crisis, the Government reversed its pro-natalist agenda in favour of what is referred to as pro-family one. [25]

As a result, the ban on family planning was lifted, clinics began distributing contraceptives and family planning advice. State assistance was reduced for families with more than three children as was maternity leave. Vasectomies were encouraged and in 1992, the abortion law was amended to allow for abortions in the case of foetal defects or risk to mother's life under the guidance of doctor in the first trimester. [26]

In the fall of 1991, the minimum age for marriage-which earlier had been reduced to 13 for females and 15 for males-was raised to 15 and 18, respectively, making marriage below those ages legal only with a court's permission. [27] In addition, Health Minister Reza Malekzadeh announced, effective July 1992, punitive measures devised to discourage large families. [28] To obtain, marriage license, it was made compulsory for the couples to attend a marriage seminar that included family planning. Additional family based initiatives were introduced during this period to promote social and family harmony amidst the changing domestic social, economic and political climate. Female sponsored programs to re-educate men and women on maintaining harmonious relationship in the family domain. Emphasis was placed on the concept of partnership between husband and wife rather than that of male guardianship enshrined in the civil code.

Economics and Finance Minister Mohammad Javad Iravani has also spoken out on the need to discourage large families. In 1990, the deputy health minister announced plans to import large quantities of contraceptives for free distribution to women in health centres, and promised that hospitals and health centres would sterilize women free of charge. Educational plans have been announced to raise public awareness of the consequences of population growth. The *Badr* Health Clinic has mobilized a corps of women volunteers to go door-to-door in poorer neighbourhoods to instruct women on the drawbacks of having too many children and persuade them to use the clinic's facilities. [29]

The government tried to raise general knowledge and understanding of population questions rather than limit its focus to promoting contraceptives. Political and religious leaders frequently address the importance of family planning in nationally televised speeches, and particularly in Friday sermons which publicly define the government's political and ideological lines. In collaboration with religious leaders, the regime employed two major strategies. First, they launched a national consensus-building campaign on population control. Religious leaders and experts used accessible language to show the importance of self-sufficiency for an independent nation, so that it would not become a slave to the whims of imperialist powers. Secondly, they incorporated family planning into the larger national health programme and recognized women's central role as active agents and decision-makers regarding their fertility, despite the political risk that such an approach poses for the 'Islamic' regime'. [30]

The family planning mission is defined in such a way that its most important function is to empower families/parents to create the kind of family they wish to have. The backbone of this policy is to prevent unwanted pregnancies and genetic abnormalities, and enable parents to space their children, as well as prevent the negative impact on women's health of too frequent pregnancies, treat infertility, and improve the general health of society by promoting the psychological and physical development of children and families. The statistics for annual population growth rate show that the government's population control policy was successful. From 3.4 percent annual growth rate in 1986, it came down to 2.7 percent in 1992 to 1.8 percent in 1995. [31]

3.1.5 Marriage and Divorce: In 1992, divorce laws were amended to curtail men's right to divorce their wives at will. The High Judicial Council agreed with a new clause in marriage law, stating that woman at the time of marriage may request that the clause 'condition under the marriage law' be included in their marriage contract. Under this clause, the bride had the right to refuse the husband the right to marry other women, and have custody of her children etc. A man no longer had the unilateral right to divorce his wife by simply by registering his will at a registry office without the woman's knowledge; men and women had to go to the civil courts for divorce and registry offices could register divorce only with a civil court's decree. [32] In addition, women and children deprived of male support were offered a measure of financial support.

The *Ojrat-ol mesal* campaign (wages for housework law) that was started in 1991 became law in December 1992 despite the considerable opposition by the conservative members of Parliament. The new law stated that if marriage contract failed to include the wealth sharing provision, then the husband must pay his wife wages for household performed during the marriage. [33] Similar reform allowed female lawyers to practice family law in the civil courts, "the law stated that in each civil court a woman who has knowledge of the law must be present to deal with divorce cases". Another major reform for women was the *Mehrieh/mahr* law, which is written into marriage contract, regarding payment to the woman on divorce or after husband's death is to be index linked with Central Bank of Iran specialists calculating the updated rate of *mahr.* [34] In October 1996, the fifth Islamic *Majles* approved a motion presented by women deputies to create the Special Commission of Women's and Family's Affairs composed of thirteen members, nine of which were women. The Commission aims at reforming laws to improve the protection of women's rights. [35]

One of the hallmarks of the Iranian Revolution in its early days was its insistence on the public separation of the sexes. The early revolutionaries not only enforced the public veiling of women, but also segregated schools, swimming pools, public transport, and even parks. Couples walking together in public were frequently accosted by *komitehs (*committees) or paramilitary enforcers of public morality known as *Khaharan-e Zeynab* (Sisters of Zeynab), and required to produce evidence that they were married or otherwise related.

Against that background, *President Rafsanjani's pronouncements in November 1990 on the subject of male-female relations were startling. During a Friday sermon, "he laid out a new road map for sexual conduct, saying that to be good Muslims young people need not "live...in a state where their desires are suppressed*". [36] *He said it was 'Iranian culture', not the Qur'an or 'Islamic ethics', that had sanctioned such repression in the past. While warning against being 'promiscuous like the Westerners' he suggested mut'a* [37] *as the Islamic alternative, not only for young people, but for the many women "who are without guardians-widows, divorcees, and those who have not yet married. He further said that registering a mut'a was not necessary, but would be desirable "if there are children*". He added that *mut'a* was sanctioned by Islamic ethics. Historically, *mut'a* principal function has been to contain human sexual needs within a legal and moral framework. [38]

Rafsanjani's speech provoked a strident public debate, with articles in magazines, editorials in newspapers, and letters from readers. A female *Majles* deputy condemned *mut'a* as a way of exploiting women and Hojiatolislam Seyyed Baqer Kharrazi, denounced it as promoting "premarital relations". [39] Many women strongly objected to the legal practice of *mut'a* on the basis of Iranian conservative ethos, particularly men's attitudes toward virginity and premarital sex. According to a woman interviewed by Fariba Adelkhah, "Such an arrangement would be ill-thought of for a young girl. It would ruin her reputation, and then no one would want her as a permanent wife. Social disapproval extends as well to widows and divorcees, even though there are many women...for whom it would be a good arrangement". [40]

3.1.6 Hejab: Ever since the imposition of mandatory hejab by Khomeini's government, Iranian women have subverted the regime with daily instances of *bad-hejabi*, which consists of women showing bits of their hair, wearing short and tight robes, using brightly coloured headscarves instead of the preferred dark blue or black, and wearing make-up or having manicured nails. The punishment for neglecting to follow Islamic rules of dress can be jail or corporal punishment, but no matter how many women the regime has arrested or how many affidavits of wrong-doing they have forced them to sign, *bad-hejabi* has become institutionalized with greater numbers of women flouting Islamic propriety for personal autonomy. [41]

Under President Rafsanjani, women took advantage of the somewhat freer atmosphere, evident under Rafsanjani's administration, to relax their observance of *hejab.* They started using brighter colours, patterned stockings, and occasionally, even lipstick. They no longer had to fear flogging or imprisonment as they had in the early 1980s before the *komitehs*-who rigorously enforced the dress code and the ban on alcohol and western popular music-were merged with the police and gendarmerie and lost their freedom of action. At most, women could expect a reprimand and fine for violating the dress code. They adopted more stylish, colourful *roopooshs,* also known as manteaux, the Islamic tunics worn over trousers-an innovation that sprang from the impracticality of the chador, which needs to be held in place. Some women gradually replaced the *maqna'eh* , a black head cover designed to be worn with a *roopoosh*, with brightly coloured shawls that revealed more hair. [42]

3.1.7 Political Participation of Women: Rafsanjani's relatively liberal and reformist policy impacted positively on women's participation in the political process of the country. An office for women's issues was set up under president Rafsanjani and Shahla Habibi was appointed as advisor to the President for women's affairs. In 1995, the government announced the appointment of a woman as deputy health minister. All ministries and provincial governments were instructed to set up offices for women's affairs. [43] In the fourth *Majles* elections (1992) the number of women doubled to reach a total of nine (or 3.3 percent). [44] Moreover, for the first time, four women were elected from the provinces, the rest five were elected from Tehran. In the fifth Majles elections, in 1996, 320 women announced their candidacy for the Majles, 179 of these were approved by Guardian Council to run in the elections; 14 were elected into the 290 member body. [45] Such a large number of female participation was unprecedented in the Iranian history.

3.1.8 Press and Women: During President Rafsanjani era the media while still under strict control experienced a gradual flourishing. The liberal Culture Minister, Mohammad Khatami who served from 1989 to 1992 approved permits for many new publications. The number of newspapers and journals doubled from 102 in 1988 to 369 in 1992. [46] The result was a plethora of women's magazines covering a wide range of issues including politics, religion, family-life, sewing, sports, health, etc...Some of the most popular of these journals included *Zanan, Farzaneh, Neda, and Jens-Dovom*. Even the religious establishment stepped into the fray by publishing *Payam-e Zan*, a woman's magazine published by a seminary in Qom with an editorial board composed exclusively of men. [47] The aim of these magazines was to promote women's status through emphasizing legal, social and economic shortcomings, and to propose changes in civil and penal laws, the employment legislation and constitutional law.

3.1.9 Voices of Reform: The climate of political liberalization marked by greater tolerance of intellectual debate and discussions paved the way for the development of a new breed of reformist Islamic intellectuals. Prominent among them were Mohsen Saidzadeh, Muhammad Mojtahed Shabestari, Mohsen Kadivar, Hassan Yousef Eshkevari and Abdolkarim Soroush. These scholars revised the use of dynamic jurisprudence or *feqh-e pooya* as opposed to relying on traditional jurisprudence or *feqh-e sonnati* that the Islamic establishment relies upon. The novelty in the approach of these scholars was that they sought to reinterpret the religious Islamic principles in the context of universal discourse of human rights and shifted the debate from traditional or historical Islam's emphasis on duties to the modernist and universal notion of rights. This method opened up Islamic jurisprudence to new solutions in response to modern problems.

Dynamic jurisprudence is particularly important because it opens jurisprudence to influence and change. Moreover, they argue that, in determining the dictates of Islam, the general principles of humanity and morality must take precedence over 'specific provisions found in various sources of Islamic jurisprudence—provisions which they generally contend were intended for, or are a product of, a different time, place and social context'. In other words, these intellectuals have argued that Shari'a should be time and place sensitive and that the provisions advocated by the Islamic Republic were largely written for a different time, place, and social context. [48]

Abdolkarim Souroush's discourse profoundly challenged the ideological foundations of Islamic Republic. He distinguished between religion and religious knowledge. *He argued that Qur'an and Hadith are part of divine and eternal religion, the interpretation of these texts is a matter of human religious knowledge, in fact is thoroughly human and this-worldly, and hence time- and context-bound.* [49] *As he explains, 'That is why the medieval version of Islam has to be sharply different from the modern version, and that is why the modern versions have to be different from each other according to the context...and this is also why religious knowledge...not being divine by virtue of its subject matter, is open to [debate and] criticism*'. [50]

Through this analysis, Soroush in effect called into question the ideological foundation of the Islamic Republic as well as the Ulema's monopoly of interpreting religion. He saw democracy and human rights as essential components of contemporary religious knowledge and argued that these principles must be integrated into Iranian society. Such statements led to his marginalization and ultimate voluntary exile as conservatives targeted him. But his writings helped women activists to frame their gender discourse within an Islamic paradigm. [51] The following statement by Shahla Sherkat, the editor in chief of Zanan, one of the leading women's magazines, clearly reveals this influence, "*Radical legal changes are needed to solve women's problems. Many articles of the civil code are based on the Shari'a, which must, therefore, be reinterpreted. Moreover, women should be involved in this undertaking. Our understanding of religion varies in each historical period, and religious interpretations should account for factors of time and space...Referring to Souroush's works, she affirms that 'through their works, some religious intellectuals have posited the necessity of radical reforms in religious thought. If they succeed, these reforms will undoubtedly be expanded to women's issues*". [52]

3.2 Khatami Period

The Khatami regime [1997-2005] continued the pace of reform that was unleashed during the period of President Rafsanjani in more vigorous manner. The day of his election in 1997 is known among Iranians as the *hamaseh-ye dovvom-e khordad* or the Epic of May 23. [53] The Epic refers to a major shift in the political discourse and an attempt to bring about tolerance and moderation in the domestic arena while improving the image of Iran abroad and ending a long period of international isolation. Women's votes were decisive in the outcome of the 1997 and 2001 presidential election, in which Khatami was elected. It may be noted that it was the first time in the annals of the Islamic Republic that gender issues prominently figured in the presidential election. Equally significant was the expansion of press and social freedoms that generated a burst of social, economic and political activities among women.

Khatami openly recognized that women's issues were controlled by a male chauvinist attitude, yet he sought to eliminate "male supremacy" offering women a presence in political, religious and social forums. [54] *As he stated, "we should have a comprehensive view of the role of women and before anything else, should not regard women as second class citizen...We should all believe that both men and women have the capability to be active in all fields, and I emphasize, in all fields*". [55]

Further he clearly recognized the 'dual responsibility' imposed on the Iranian woman and sought a balance between the two. *According to him, "we want a woman who is the pivot of the home to be the manager and master of the house. At the same time, there should be absolutely no reduction in her social responsibilities and active presence in society"*. [56] *He added that the central role of the woman at home should not marginalize her from public life, while her presence in the social arena should not lead to the deterioration of the family and the undermining of its strength and stability. He furthermore points to the inherent difference between men and women, without bestowing an inferior or superior status on either one. He rejects both male and female domination and instead advocates the leadership of the competent and meritorious, regardless of sex*. [57]

It was this approach of President Khatami that helped women to participate with more confidence and freedom in the national public life of Iran. The Second Development Plan (1994-98) which had already been issued when Khatami assumed the presidential office—briefly touched on the issue of female education by stating the following as a goal, 'Paying attention to the education of girls and the literacy training of women and young mothers'. The 2001 National Report on Women's Status in the Islamic Republic of Iran, published by the Centre for Women's Participation (*Markaz Mosharekat Zanan*), clarified the female education priorities of the period covered by the Third Development Plan (1999-2003). This document reflected the concerns of its time and demonstrated a deep transformation in the approach to gender and education. It viewed education as a woman's basic human right and called for increased gender sensitivity in all aspects of schooling. The Report specified the following as the priorities of female education: [58]

1. Revising existing education laws that are gender biased.
2. Reducing gender gaps in the fields of science, mathematics and applied sciences.
3. Modifying educational materials in order to portray the correct image of women's roles in the family and society, and of the mutual rights of women, men and the family at all levels.
4. Emphasising the participation of female specialists in planning and policy making at all levels of education.
5. Developing and promoting counselling services in high schools to prepare and guide students towards more appropriate fields of study in order to eliminate the concentration of female university students in certain degrees.
6. Determining a particular quota for creating equal opportunities for women in a number of specific university degrees.
7. Teaching management skills to women with the aim of enhancing their participation in the sphere of decision-making.
8. Expanding and diversifying technical and vocational training programmes for women with a view to creating employment opportunities.

3.2.1 Participation in Education and Economy: Under Khatami, special priority was given to policies that empowered and expanded women's opportunities. As a consequence the participation of women in the higher education increased tremendously. To this effect a large number of seminars and conferences were organized on the issues related to rights and status of women with a view to promote them. In 2000, the sixth Parliament reformed the education law allowing unmarried female students to study abroad. [59] Also in 2000, the first women's studies institute, The Iranian Society for Women's Studies was established. In 2001, through the efforts of women's rights advocates in Iran, Allameh Tabatabai University, Tarbiat Modares University, and Al Zahra University started women's studies programme at the master's level and shortly thereafter Tehran University organized a similar programme. [60] Zahra Rahnavard, wife of former prime minister was appointed as the chancellor of the women's Al Zahra University. She is the first woman in Iranian history to head a university. [61]

The most tangible measure undertaken by the Ministry of Education to reduce gender bias in schools was the revision of certain textbook pictures during 2002-03 in order to portray more girls engaged in traditionally 'male-orientated' tasks, especially in the technical-vocational fields. [62] In 1998, more women than men were admitted to the competitive national university entrance examinations. [63] In 1999, the percentage of females attending university surpassed the number of men for the first time since the revolution. The admission rate for females was about four per cent higher than for male students. [64]

The Tehran Bureau of education announced in July 2000 that elementary school students were now allowed to wear "bright, happy colours" in place of traditional black. According to the Bureau's directive the new policy is to brighten the mood and raise hope among students and preserve their psychological health. "Happy, Bright colours include pink, blue, beige, light green and yellow". But the Bureau was quick to exclude loud and gaudy colours or dress cuts that are "beneath the dignity of education environment". [65]

The office for Women's Affairs in the Ministry of Agriculture also implemented many projects for rural women. Thousands of women were trained in special courses. [66] During this period, a few women have occupied high positions such as vice presidents, deputy ministers, regional governors and regional deputy governors. There was a significant change from previous periods where women did not hold any of these roles. But women's participation in higher levels of employment such as leadership, managerial and decision making positions did not increase more than 2.7 percent. [67]

The impact of gender oriented policy of Rafsanjani and Khatami became visible by the end of 2000. Thus, with respect to literacy, illiterates as a percentage of Iranian women aged fifteen to twenty-four have declined from over one-third in 1980 to less than one-tenth in 2000. Over the same period, the illiteracy rate for the entire population of adult women has been cut in half, from about 60 percent to about 30 percent.

As for education, the number of women in secondary school as a percentage of the eligible age group (the only participation in education figure for which data from both 1980 and 2000 is readily available) more than doubled from about 30 percent to almost 80 percent (The corresponding figure for young men also increased but not as dramatically). As of 1999, for every 100 boys in primary school, 96 girls were enrolled, indicating that boys and girls were almost equally likely to be learning basic literacy and numeracy skills. In 2000, half of all Iranian university students were women, as were 60 percent of entering students, who were selected on the basis of a difficult nationwide exam. Similarly gain for women in economic field also became visible.

Thus Women in 2005 make up 27 percent of the Iranian labour force, up from 20 percent in 1980.According to a study published by the University of North Carolina Population Studies and Research Centre for Asia and the Pacific, the percentage of all Iranian women who are economically active has more than doubled from 6.1 percent in 1986 to 13.7

percent in 2000. With respect to family planning, "levels of childbearing have declined faster than in any other country", going from 5.6 births per woman in 1985 to 2.0 in 2000, a drop accomplished by a voluntary, but government-sponsored, birth control program. [68] In 2003, women's share of bachelor's degrees was nearly 50 percent, of master's degrees was 27 percent, and of Ph.D. degrees was 24 percent. [69]

3.2.2 Participation in Decision-Making Bodies: President Khatami took the concrete initiative to involve women in various decision making bodies of the governance ranging from national to local levels. Thus, he appointed Masoumeh Ebtekar as vice president of Environment and Zahra Shojai as his as his special advisor on women affairs. Shojai became head of his coordination body on women and the Centre for Women's Participation which was affiliated to the office of the President.

Later in 2001, Khatami nominated Zahra Rahnavard as his senior adviser on cultural affairs. The journalist, Jamileh Kadivar, wife of Minister of Culture and Islamic guidance Ataollah Mohajerani was appointed as his special advisor on press affairs. Khatami's wife, Zohreh Sadeghi, was appointed to oversee a special committee designed to address the needs of rural women. In 1997, the head of the judiciary, Muhammad Yazdi, appointed Mahindokht Daoodi as undersecretary to the office responsible for the implementation of rulings issued by family courts. All public bodies under three branches of the state—the judiciary, the legislature and the executive—were instructed to establish a Women Cell to advise them on women related issues. Khatami also maintained each ministerial office and provincial governor's office for women's affairs established by Rafsanjani. Further Zahra Shojai, implemented a plan for the decentralization of provincial governance where a 12 member committee of women in each province, would 336 women to government posts. [70]

Earlier, in 1998, Khatami announced the establishment of the first women's police academy. The graduates would serve throughout regular police units. [71] While the ban against women serving as judges was not lifted, women judicial rights were extended to serve as investigative magistrates or consulting judges. At the same time, women were given licenses to open and head notary offices, a profession conventionally held by men. [72] Further, the female civil servants were allowed to retire after twenty years of service.

3.2.3 Political Participation: The percentage of seats held by women during the four parliamentary terms increased from just two per cent in the Third Majles (1988-91), to five percent in the Sixth Majles (2000-04). However, it declined slightly in the first year of the Seventh Majles (2004-2008). [73] At the same time, the number of female parliamentarians increased to 14 in the mid-term parliamentary in 1997. [74] Seven women attempted to run in the Assembly of Experts election in 1998. All the candidates were rejected based upon their lack of religious qualification. Women also participated in the Municipal local elections, held for the first time in February 1999. An estimated 5,000 women were approved by Guardian Council to run for 220,000 positions throughout the country and 300 of them won. [75]

Officials of the Women's Bureau of the Ministry of Interior organized and promoted across Iran more than 100 workshops and seminars to encourage the participation of women. The Centre for Women's Participation was created by Khatami to promote women's rights as part of the President's office. [76] During the period 1999-2001, the number of women who occupied high positions within formal politics increased. The number of seats in parliament held by women increased to 4.1 percent. Three women were advisers to the president; sixteen women were advisers to different ministries; there were 106 women in the position of directorship. However, women were on the whole under-represented in formal politics. [77]

3.2.4 Women's Participation in Sports: Championed by Faizeh Hashemi, the youngest daughter of former President

Hashemi Rafsanjani, Iranian women have ignored Islamic propriety and argued for separate facilities for indoor activities as well as the right to engage in outdoor activities, such as bicycle riding as long as they are properly dressed. In 1998, thousands of women broke a long-time barrier preventing women from attending sporting events when they poured into Tehran's stadium to greet the Iranian soccer team after it qualified for the 1998 World Cup, which resulted in special sections of the stadium being designated for female spectators. In 2000, Tehran had 85 women's basketball teams and over two million women were participating in soccer, basketball, swimming, tennis, skiing, etc…compared to only ten thousand women who engaged in sports on the eve of the revolution. [78] By 2004, the number of women athletes was estimated at more than 1.2 million. [79] They received training from 32,000 women coaches in 10,000 public and private sports centre. [80]

3.2.5 Freedom of Press: Under his Presidency, Iran witnessed tremendous expansion of civil society and freedom of expression. Earlier when he served as Ministry of Culture under President Rafsanjani he had brought significant change cultural change. He continued the same policy with more intensity and commitment. As a result many women's magazines sprang up. Faezeh Hashemi's newspaper *Zan* provided social and political news. *Huquq-e-Zanan* (Women's rights) was the first magazine devoted exclusively to female legal matters. [81] In 1998, Jamileh Kadivar, a journalist and a Member of Parliament (2000 -2004) established the Women Journalists' Trade Association and in 2002 published Women's Voice (*Seday-e Zan*).

In 1999, no less than 15 journals were devoted to women's issues. [82] Prior to 1979 there were no women publishers in Iran. By the late 1990s there were over 400. While these publications thrived in more open environment created by Khatami, they generated opposition from conservatives. *Salam, Tous* and *Jameeh* were closed down and Hashemi and *Zanan* publisher Shahla Sherkat summoned to answer charges of slander. [83]

Khatami's presidency also provided Iranians with a sense of freedom in the public sphere. Men and women experienced greater freedom of movement, to mingle on university campuses and throughout towns and parks. The streets became vibrant and colourful as women exchanged their black veils for bright coloured scarves. [84] They also began wearing more make up and exposing more skin. In return, the state returned the moral squads to the streets forcing women to adhere to conservative dress. Western-style modern coffee shops were opened rapidly throughout major cities. New modern shopping centres emerged that soon became the centre for young people to gather, socialize and spend time together. These businesses were particularly not tolerated before 1997 as one of their functions was to provide a mean for inter-gender relationships. [85]

Another progress for women was the sharp increase in the number of women's NGOs after 1997. In an effort to connect the government with people, President Khatami initiated a program which supported establishment of NGOs. [86] Having public support, the program attracted many intellectuals and youths. In less than 5 years, the number of NGOs tripled and in some areas that political/social activity were inhibited numerous NGOs started operating and giving service to individual women. These NGOs promoted women's confidence and created opportunities for them to seek new employment and enter new areas of social activity. In 1997, there were only 67 women NGOs; in 2005 this figure increased to 337. [87]

In addition to above fields Khatami's reformist policies empowered women in many inter-personal areas. For instance Parliament revised the child custody law in 1998 which changed that the custody could no longer be awarded to an unfit father, if the father was a drug addict, an alcoholic or "morally corrupt". [88] However the process of reform was slowed down during Khatami's second term partly on account of opposition by the conservative dominated Islamic establishment, particularly, the *Majles* and Council of Guardians (a body that can review, veto, or mandate revision of legislation).

Despite Khatami's best efforts many other important reformist bills related to women could not get passed by the *Majles* and become law in the land. Important among them are proposal related to create a *Majles* Commission to address issues relating to family, youth and women, and a plan to give the right of residence and nationality to non-Iranian spouses of Iranian women were either rejected or severely revised by the Supreme Leader, Guardian Council or Expediency Council. [89] Similarly the UN Convention on Elimination of All Discriminations against Women (CEDAW), though ratified by *Majles* with some reservations was vetoed in (2001) by Council of Guardians. The latter rejected the proposed law on the grounds that it conflicted with several principles of the constitution and Islam, including inheritance and divorce laws, the *hejab* and polygamy. [90] This was indeed a serious setback to many women organisations and individual personalities in Iran who had worked actively to convince the ruling elite to accede to the United Nations Convention for the Elimination of All Forms of Discrimination against Women, while respecting the principles of Islam.

A conservative backlash against Khatami's reforms has also produced two laws that women regard as retrograde. The first, an amendment to the Press Law, makes it a punishable crime to print pictures or material that will "exploit" women, insult women, encourage women to "ornamentation", or further friction between men and women. The second law mandates a segregated health care delivery system, in which medical practitioners are permitted to treat only members of their own sex. Both bills were approved against the opposition of Khatami's government, women activists, and women's magazines. The medical bill was also opposed by many doctors. It was originally sent back to parliament by the

Council of Guardians on the grounds that the government lacked the funds to create a two-track health care delivery system. [91]

Notwithstanding these setbacks Khatami remained unflagging in his support of civil society and women's rights which is evident from his statement which he made as late as in 2003 despite the pressure of conservative factions: "*in early years of revolution we made restrictions for our female students to enter universities which led to sharp decline in their progress. Then restrictions were gradually removed. As a result we witnessed the growth in the women's participation in higher education at a remarkable rate. In 2000, 60 percent of students who entered universities were female. This may be neither ideal nor natural. But I believe that in the near future it will reach its balance. We have to let this equilibrium to be restored naturally. It is not justifiable to artificially create obstacles and to reduce their participation in higher education. Current circumstances demonstrate that women face more restrictions and deprivations than young men. The best way is to open the higher education system at various levels to women and remove the quota system in courses such as mining, engineering and the medical disciplines*". [92]

Under his presidency, non-governmental organizations expanded to an unprecedented degree, and the social environment grew less strained so that women moved with greater freedom in the public sphere holding meetings, publishing, making films and suffering less harassment for clothing choices. In particular, during Khatami's term the preparations for, and celebrations of, International Women's Day became a rallying point that brought women of all political and religious persuasions together. However during his tenure, women gained a much larger role in government and in the workplace, as well as a greater presence in the public space.

Endnotes

1. On factional politics in Iran, see Moslem, Mehdi (2002), "Factional Politics in Post-Khomeini Iran", Syracuse: University

Press.

2. Povey, Elaheh Rostami, "Women and Work in Iran, part 1, available at: http://www.stateofnature.org/?p=5243.
3. Tazmini, Ghoncheh, "Khatami's Iran: The Islamic Republic and the Turbulent Path to Reform", p. 66, I.B. Tauris Publishers.
4. Ramazani, Nesta (1993), "Women in Iran: The Revolutionary Ebb and Flow", *Middle East Journal,* Vol. 47, No. 3, p. 412.
5. Vakil, Sanam (2012), "Women and Politics in the Islamic Republic of Iran: Action and Reaction", p. 111, Bloomsbury Academic.
6. Aryan, Khadijeh (2012), "The Boom in Women's Education", in Tara Povey and Elaheh Rostami Povey (eds.), 'Women, Power and Politics in the 21st Century Iran', p. 41, Ashgate Publishing Limited.
7. Ramazani, No. 4, p. 413.
8. Ibid.
9. Ibid.
10. Kian, Azadeh (1997), "Women and Politics in Post-Islamist Iran: the Gender Conscious Drive to Change", *British Journal of Middle Eastern Studies,* Vol. 24, No. 1, p. 84.
11. Ibid.
12. Bahramitash, Roksana (2003), "Islamic Fundamentalism and Women's Economic Role: The Case of Iran", *International Journal of Politics, Culture, and Society,* Vol. 16, No. 4, p. 563.
13. Ibid.
14. The above facts and data have taken from Kian, No.10, p. 95.
15. For the above data see Bahramitash, No. 12, p. 562.
16. Poya, Maryam (1999), "Women, Work and Islamism: Ideology and Resistance in Iran", p. 98, Zed Books: London.
17. Ibid.
18. Ibid., p. 115.
19. Ibid., p. 117.
20. Ibid., p. 113.
21. For the above fact and data see Poya, No. 16. pp. 114-119.
22. Ibid., p. 120.
23. Ibid., p. 121.
24. Vakil, No. 5, p. 113.
25. Pro-natalist policy refers to the policy of increasing the child bearing. Ayatollah Khomeini viewed family planning as western

practice. Therefore, he immediately dismantled such a reform and did not advocate for contraception. He saw a large population as an advantage during war with Iraq (1980-1988). During war, Ayatollah called for "soldiers for Islam" and encouraged women to have more children.

26. Vakil, No. 5, p. 114.
27. Ramazani, No. 4, p. 415.
28. Ibid.
29. For the above data see Ramazani, No. 4, p. 415.
30. For the above data see Hoodfar, Homa (1996), "Bargaining with Fundamentalism: Women and the Politics of Population Control in Iran", *Reproductive HealthMatters,* Vol. 4, No. 8, pp. 31-32.
31. Ibid., p. 33.
32. For the above data see Poya, No. 16, pp. 101-102.
33. Vakil, No. 5, p. 114.
34. For the above data see Poya, No. 16, p. 101.
35. Kian, No. 10, p. 95.
36. Ramazani, No. 4, p. 419.
37. Mut'a, practiced only by Shi'i Muslims, allows a man to take a sigheh (temporary wife) as his legal spouse for any length of time agreed to by the couple upon the payment of a mahr. At the end of the agreed time, the marriage ends automatically, without divorce, unless renewed. Any children from the union are legitimate heirs of the father.
38. Ramazani, No. 4, p. 419.
39. Ibid., p. 420.
40. Ibid.
41. Bayat, Asef (2007), "A Women's Non-Movement: What It Means to Be a Woman Activist in an Islamic State", *Comparative Studies of South Asia, Africa and the Middle East,* Vol. 27, No. 1, p. 165.
42. For the above data see Ramazani, No. 4, pp. 421-423.
43. Vakil, No. 5, p. 124.
44. Kian, No. 10, p. 84.
45. Vakil, No. 5, p. 126.
46. Ibid., p. 121.
47. Kian, No. 10, p. 93.
48. For the above data see Razavi, Shahra (2006), "Islamic Politics, Human Rights and Women's claims for Equality in Iran", *Third World Quaterly,* Vol. 27, No. 7, pp. 1226-1229.

49. Vakil, No. 5, p. 106.
50. Razavi, No. 48, p. 1227.
51. Vakil, No. 5, p. 106.
52. Kian, No. 10, p. 91.
53. Mehran, Golnar (2003), "Khatami, Political Reform and Education in Iran", *Comparative Education,* Vol. 39, No. 3, p. 311.
54. Ibid.
55. Ibid.
56. Mehran, No. 53, p. 318.
57. Ibid.
58. For the above data, see Tazmini, No. 3, p. 67.
59. Vakil, No. 5, p. 111.
60. Ibid.
61. Tazmini, No. 3, p. 68.
62. Ibid.
63. Ibid.
64. Ibid., p. 69.
65. Shahidian, Hammed (2002), "Gender Politics in Islamic Republic", p. 198, Greenwood Press, London.
66. Koolaee, Elaheh (2012), "Women in the Parliament", in Tara Povey and Elaheh Rostami Povey (eds.), 'Women, Power and Politics in 21st Century Iran', p. 140, Ashgate Publishing Limited.
67. Nejadbahram, Zahra (2012), "Women and Employment", in Tara Povey and Elaheh Rostami Povey (eds.), 'Women, Power and Politics in 21st Century Iran', p. 84, Ashgate Publishing Limited.
68. The data in the above paragraph has been taken from Halper, Louis (2005), "Law and Women's Agency in Post-Revolutionary Iran", *Harvard Journal of Law and Gender*, Vol. 28, pp. 90-91.
69. Rezai, Goli M., "The Future of Iran: Educational Reform Women and Education in the Islamic Republic of Iran: Repressive Policies, Unexpected Outcomes", available at: http://www.li.com/docs/default-source/default-document-library/women-and-education-in-the-islamic-republic-of-iran-repressive-policies-unexpected-outcomes.
70. For the above data, see Vakil, No. 5, pp. 141-143.
71. Ibid., p. 142.

72. Ibid., p. 143.
73. Tazmini, No. 3, p. 69.
74. Vakil, No. 5, p. 142.
75. Ibid., p. 143.
76. Ibid., p. 141.
77. Povey, Elaheh (2001), "Feminist Contestation of Institutional Domain in Iran", *Feminist Review,* No. 69, p. 52.
78. Robin Wright, "Iran's New Revolution", *Foreign Affairs,* January/February 2000, available at: http://fullaccess.foreignaffairs.org/20000101faessay10/robin-writght/iran-s-new- revolution.html.
79. Afary, Janet (2009), "Sexual Politics in Iran", p. 333, Cambridge University Press.
80. Ibid.
81. Vakil, No. 5, p. 143.
82. Tazmini, No. 3, p. 69.
83. Vakil, No. 5, p. 143.
84. Ibid.
85. Majbouri, Mehdi, "On the Dynamics of Women's Rights Movement in Iran, 1996-2006", available at : http://faculty.babson.edu/mmajbouri/documents/papers/womenrights.pdf.
86. Ibid.
87. Koolaee, No. 66, p. 140.
88. Halper, No. 68, p. 95.
89. Ibid., p. 149.
90. Afary, No. 79, p. 330.
91. Ibid.
92. Aryan, No. 6, pp. 42-43.

4

Islam, State and Gender Discourse: Ahmadinejad Period (2005-2013)

Unlike the Rafsanjani and Kḥatami government's reformist approach, Mahmoud Ahmadinejad government adopted a hard line, conservative approach to women. As a result many of the gains that women had achieved in the field of education, marriage, health, employment opportunities and political participation under the previous two regimes either received serious jolt.

During his 2005 presidential campaign Ahmadinejad even did not mention gender as a part of his political platform. During his campaign for presidency in 2005, when asked about *bad hejabi* (laxity in women's dress) he stressed that *'Hejab' (the Islamic clothing that covers the body from head to toe) is not an issue, especially in light of economic and social problems facing the Islamic Republic.* [1] President's first deputy repeatedly announced that the, "new government has not expressed any commitments towards a new strategy for improving women's conditions. Women's status was not on top of President Ahmadinejad agenda during his presidential campaign in 2005, thus the new government feels no commitment towards this matter." [2] The issue of women rights was also very much missing in Ahmadinejad's Presidential Campaign of 2009.

His government advanced the notion of 'gender equilibrium' and 'appropriate gender roles' as an essential component of social stability. Resurrecting the initial pro-natalist views of Ayatollah Khomeini, he encouraged women to return to their natural role as nurturers. New governmental programmes and publications stressed traditional interpretations of female issues, emphasizing the role of women as mothers and downplaying female participation in the workplace and even in politics. The approach was very much reflected in the government's decision to change the name of the Centre for Women's Participation as the Centre for Women and Family Affairs in 2005, immediately after assuming the office of Presidency.

The addition of the word 'family' indicated the direction in which his administration hoped to take women's issues. It once again emphasized women's identification with the family and the idea that her social identity depends on marriage and family. The conservative head of the Centre, Tabib Zadeh Nouri, appointed by Ahmadinejad, was quick to announce that Iran is no longer committed to international treaties such as 1995 Beijing Platform for Action. She denounced it 'western treaty' which, according to her, aimed at "corrupting Iranian women and destroying Islamic values". [3] *"So long as I am alive", she declared, "I won't allow Iran to join CEDAW or any other international treaty for women*". [4] She also ordered the elimination of several studies on women's issues done by the Centre for Women's Participation. The budget for governmental institutions affecting women was significantly reduced. [5] Many NGOs were closed as the government viewed them with suspicion, associating them with western ideas and interests.

Since 2005, several women's organizations and publications have been shut down, including *Zanan*. Like Ayatollah Khomeini and the Shah, Ahmadinejad considered that gender relations were the key to social change. He wanted the end of the western cultural influence in Iran, which was symbolized in hejab and youth appearance. He established the "Islamic guidance police force" which during his administration has arrested and prosecuted thousands of women across the country for not wearing proper Islamic clothing. [6] Less than a year into his first term there was a noticeable uptick in the state's efforts to banish *bad hejabi* from the streets. [7] While the general female population was subjected to more stringent vigilance in response to the government 'morality' campaign, more specifically, the government targeted activist women and particularly secular ones who initiated and actively participated in direct confrontation with the government. More women's rights activists were serving terms in jail under Ahmadinejad than at any time in the history of the Islamic Republic. [8]

4.1 Women's Education

Ahmadinejad government created a 'special council for development and Promotion of Humanities'. The council appointed seven humanities scholars and the main task of the council was to oversee the islamisation of the disciplines. A number of professors were asked to retire or were dismissed because they did not support the new policy. [9] In April 2008, the government announced its intention to limit acceptance of female students in specific fields of university study. It announced 60 percent of university seats to male students and forty percent to female students, even if their grades are higher than male students. [10] The program which seeks to redress the disproportionately high number of female university students drew attention to government's gender bias. While no official legislation has been submitted or passed but in February 2008, the *Sazeman Sanjesh* (government admission organization), stated that it had already been enforcing a de facto quota system restricting female admission since 2006. [11] The organization leaders acknowledged that they had been promoting a male priority acceptance policy.

In 2008, the *Majles* Research Centre, which was in the hands of Ahmadinejad supporters, published a report that expressed 'concern' over the increased number of women in higher education. It called this increase "a waste of the country's resources for educating professionals" and a way "to severely damage the family institution" which would result in an unstable society. [12] This kind of policies negatively affects women's education and employment status and opportunities.

Both the Ministry of Education (Elementary and

secondary Education) and the Ministry of Science and Technology, attempted gender segregation by limiting or restricting women's access to some 77 fields of study. Most restrictions were published in the annual manual of the Ministry of Science, Research and Technology, which regulates higher education in Iran. The manual stated the available fields of study for women and men. In that, each individual university imposed its own restrictions based on gender—36 public universities banned women from studying in 77 fields of study that included technical and applied science majors, political science, computer science, business and engineering etc. These fields are more prestigious and have a higher probability of access to job markets and higher paying jobs. Interestingly, neither these universities nor the minister of science, Research, and Technology have explained why they restricted choices and adopted the process of 'single-gendering'. [13]

Since September 2009, female students have been required to study at the universities in their towns or cities, thereby restricting their free access to higher education. No such requirement exists for male students. *Mousa Ghorbani, the head of the judiciary commission of parliament stated that female localization provides a solution to social problems generated, "when girls move to the other cities to study, it causes some problem for their families as well as society. If they stay with their families they help to improve the peace of society and themselves*". [14] Kamaran Daneshjoo, the then Higher Education Minister emphasized the significance of gender segregation and the establishment of quota systems that resulted in limiting women's access to some postgraduate courses and the segregation of some classes for women and men. [15] This leads to reduction in the women's choices.

The school and the university textbooks were revised to lay greater emphasis upon women's domestic roles. In terms of the number and percentage of women in higher education institutions, there seems to be a significant decline in the percentage of women due to restrictions and quota system. [16] Another reason could be high fees in private universities which female students cannot afford (Tables 4.1, 4.2 and 4.3).

Table 4.1: Total Number and Percentage of Female Students in Islamic Azad (Private) University

Year	1996-97	2001-02	2004-05	2006-07
Total	6,13,468	8,06,639	10,98,491	12,89,637
Percent	41	48	48	46

Contd...

Year	2007/08	2008/09	2009/10
Total	13,02,569	13,91,509	14,60,009
Percent	44	41	39.7

Sources: Department of Statistics and Information Technology, 2010, Tehran, Institute for Research and Planning in Higher Education; quoted in Aryan, Khadijeh (2012), "The Boom in Women's Education", in Tara Povey and Elaheh Rostami Povey (eds.), 'Women, Power and Politics in 21st Century Iran', p. 46, Ashgate Publishing Limited.

Table 4.2: Total Number and Percentage of Female Students in all Universities

Year	2000-01	2007-08	2008-09	2009-10
Total	15,66,963	33,91,852	33,49,741	37,90,859
Women	7,68,597 (49)	17,95,836 (53)	17,08,553 (51)	18,74,966 (49)

Figures in parentheses indicate percent of the total.
Source: Aryan, Khadijeh, "The Boom in Women's Education", 2012, in Tara Povey and Elaheh Rostami Povey (eds.), 'Women, Power and Politics in 21st Century Iran', p. 47, Ashgate Publishing Limited.

However, according to the Ministry of Science, Research and Technology during the 2007-2008 academic year, 51 percent of those who successfully passed the competitive national college entrance examination, *concour* [17] and were admitted to public universities in Iran were women; meanwhile female students comprised 50 percent of the total number of those studying at institutes of higher learning. For the first time in the history of higher education in Iran, in the 2009 concour, university capacity (1,500,000) exceeded the number of applicants (1,250,000). [18] The gender gap for university education was reversed during the 2007-2008 academic year, during which the admissions rate was 51 percent females and 49 percent males. Similarly, among the 108,238 students who graduated from university in that year, 49 percent were females. [19] This shows that women's demand for higher education and their success in occupying a bigger share of university places has been phenomenal.

In addition, in 2008-2009, 68 percent of Payam Noor Distance Learning University were females. [20] In 2010 and 2011, students who participated in the concour, 60 percent of them were females. [21]

Table 4.3: Total Number and Percentage of Female Students in Public Universities

Gender/Year	1996-97	2001-02	2004-05
Total Students	5,79,070	7,59,870	10,18,980
Females as percent of total	36	50	54

Contd...

Gender/Year	2005-06	2008-09	2009-10
Total Students	11,91,048	19,17,183	16,79,863
Females as percent of total	55	58	59

Sources: Department of Statistics and Information Technology, 2010, Tehran, Institute for Research and Planning in Higher Education; quoted in Aryan, Khadijeh (2012), "The Boom in Women's Education", in Tara Povey and Elaheh Rostami Povey (eds.), 'Women, Power and Politics in 21st Century Iran', p. 46, Ashgate Publishing Limited.

Table 4.4 indicates that the percentage of female students at all levels increased significantly during the 15 years from 1995-2010. It is, however, interesting to see that women's participation in secondary and higher education slightly declined. This might be as a result of some regressive policies that the Ministry of Health put in place to limit the percentage of women entering medical fields and post-graduate studies. [22]

Table 4.4: Female Students' Participation at Different Academic Levels (1995-2010)

Year	1995	2000	2005	2010
Pre-primary Total number	67,782 (48)	1,25,856 (50)	2,56,820 (52)	2,34,365 (51)
Primary Total number	45,94,053 (47)	39,38,766 (47)	29,91,211 (48)	29,30,152 (49)
Total Secondary All Programmes Total number	34,02,131 (45)	47,03,729 (47)	43,57,512 (48)	36,48,542 (45)
Total Tertiary Total number	3,84,461 (37)	6,35,973 (45)	10,83,664 (51)	18,74,966 (49.5)

Figures in parentheses indicate percent of the total.
Sources: Rezai-Rashti, Goli M., "The Future of Iran: Educational Reform Women and Education in the Islamic Republic of Iran: Repressive Policies, Unexpected Outcomes", p. 6.

4.2 Employment and Family Planning

Ahmadinejad declared that a stronger Iran, with a nuclear capability, needed to be more populous and recommended more part-time rather than full-time employment for women. More emphasis was given to the role of women within the family. New laws encouraged women to work part time and to take early retirement after twenty years of service. The government also cut the hours of women working at government agencies. Iran's Minister of Culture and Islamic Guidance, Muhammad Hossein Saffar Harandi, encouraged women to leave work early so that they can attend to their familial duties. [23]

Rather than expanding employment for women, Ahmadinejad's central policy with regard to the family was facilitating marriage through various loans and subsidies, advocating pro-natalist policies, and promoting part-time employment. In 2006, Iranian President Mahmoud Ahmadinejad's appealed to Iranian legislators to take steps to boost the country's population from 70 to 120 million and condemning the country's recent attainment of the two-child family urged Iranians to have more. [24] He disclosed vigorous support in increasing birth rates and indicated the country will benefit from an additional 50 million citizens, who would strengthen its position against the West. [25] He further called on Iranian women to return to the family home, and devote their energies to their "primary" responsibility of raising children. [26]

The policy of marriage loan was costing the state exchequer dearly. In 2007, Tehran's mayor Muhammad Baqir Qalibaf complained that he could not continue the marriage-loan program, which his predecessor Ahmadinejad had instituted as mayor, because it would bankrupt the city's treasury. However, Ahmadinejad viewed marriage loans as integral to his campaign strategy and battled with the Seventh Parliament to institute similar loans for the whole nation. In 2006, he required the sum of 1.3 billion dollars to provide cash subsidies for marriage and rent to low-income families, and established the Imam Reza Love Fund (*Sandoq-e Mehr-e Imam Reza*) for this purpose. When the Parliament refused to approve the fund, Ahmadinejad created an alternative venue, including conservative NGOs that were not responsible to the Parliament and could distribute the funds independently. [27]

In 2010, under a new plan the government allocated financial rewards for each new born baby. For each child born in the Iranian calendar beginning 21 March, 2010, the government granted, each child born will receive a deposit of $950 in a government bank account. The child will then receive $95 every year until reaching 18. Parents will be expected to pay matching amounts into the accounts. Recipients will then be permitted to withdraw the money at the age of 20 and can use it for education, marriage, health or housing. The program was expected to be especially attractive to lower-income people, who formed the backbone of Mr. Ahmadinejad's support in the presidential elections in 2005 and 2009. [28] This policy would encourage population growth and will eventually leave its impact on women's presence in society as it discourages women's social roles and emphasizes their roles within the family.

School textbooks and teachers reproduce the conservative gender roles that exist within the society. Textbooks imply that a good woman is a good mother and wife, not a good manager, an employer, a director, a trader, a politician and so on [29] which has a huge impact on women's employment. Despite their education and experience women continued to face discrimination in terms of wages and job promotions. Women are rarely offered positions such as heads of departments, deans of faculties and/or directors or chancellors of universities. As demonstrated in the table below, university faculties are highly male dominated and women occupy only 6 per cent of management positions in comparison with men. [30]

Aṣ indicated in Table 4.5, the percentage of women faculty members in 2009 was only 17.5 percent, which is still far below expectations. [31] Not only in education, the presence of women in higher positions of leadership, managerial and decision-making positions remained restricted to a small minority. Since 2005, under President Ahmadinejad this figure has decreased to 2 percent which was 2.7 percent under Khatami. [32]

Many women in their workplaces face obstacles to their upward mobility. Favourable circumstances are created for men to be promoted to higher positions, but not for women. Many women feel that they have to work harder in order to prove their counterparts that they are as good as them in the workplaces and believe that society will accept them only if they perform their household duties equally well. [33] Moreover, working women with young children were unable to afford the expense of privatized kindergartens and are compelled to sit at home.

According to the results of 2006 Iranian census, only 3.5 million Iranian women are salaried workers, compared with

23.5 million men constituting only 15 percent of workforce and well below the world average of 45 percent. Some 33 percent of Iran's female labour force is in professional jobs, concentrated in education, healthcare, and social services—hardly a seismic shift from the pre-revolutionary period in terms of gender roles. Slightly over half of all teachers in Iran are women, but the proportion of female university teaching staff is, at 20 percent and less than 4 percent of employed women are found in senior or executive or managerial positions. [34]

Table 4.5: Faculty Members in Higher Educational Institutions

	Public Universities		Islamic Azad University (Private)		Grand Total	
Year	Women	Total	Women	Total	Women	Total
1995	7,171 (18)	40,477	2,285 (13)	18,228	9,456 (16)	58,706
2009	10,414 (13)	78,490	14,590 (23)	64,642	25,004 (18)	1,43,132

Figures in parentheses indicate percent of the total.
Sources: Iran Statistical Yearbook, 2009, Tehran: Institute for Research and Planning in Higher Education; Aryan, Khadijeh, "The Boom in Women's Education", 2012, in Tara Povey and Elaheh Rostami Povey (eds.), 'Women, Power and Politics in 21st Century Iran', p. 49, Ashgate Publishing Limited.

Majority of the women work in the informal sector of the economy which includes a wide range of economic activities, ranging from self-employment, family businesses micro enterprises and home based work of various sorts as this does not require the permission of the husband. [35] In 2008, female labour participation in state enterprises was 34 percent as compared to 66 percent males. [36]

4.3 Marriage

Ahmadinejad's administration proposed a new family law to change the provisions of Family Protection Act (*Layehe*

Hemayate Khanevadeh) that was nearly passed in the conservative-controlled Eighth *Majles* in the summer of 2008, but was shelved temporarily due to an August rally of women mobilized by Iranian women activists. The bill not only rolled back the improvements in the previous family code, but also legalizes sigheh and polygamy without the consent of the husband's previous wife. Some of the controversial provisions of the proposed bill were: Article 22 [37] which removes any requirement to register temporary marriages (*sigheh*). The civil code authorizes men to enter into an infinite number of temporary marriages called sigheh, the length of which many vary from a couple of minutes to 99 years. The removal of the registration requirement in temporary marriage eliminates any financial or legal protection for women in these unions.

Secondly, Article 23 [38] of the proposed bill authorizes polygamous marriages contingent upon the financial capacity of men. It does not set specific parameters for adequate financial resources to support multiple wives, or define overall concepts of justice or equal treatment of multiple wives. Most notably absent from the Family Protection Bill is any effective requirement of consent of the first wife for her husband to enter into a second marriage. Under Islamic law, a man is entitled to marry up to four wives and many countries allow polygamy. However, Iran is one of the few countries that require the consent of the first wife before a husband can take another. Polygamy is not commonly practiced in Iranian society but the government of Ahmadinejad has pursued these amendments to enshrine traditional elements of Islamic law and advance the state's maternal image of women into the country's legal system.

Article 25 [39] imposes a tax on the *mehrieh* the wife if it exceeds the standard rates. While this amount is legally owed to the wife at the time of the marriage, women often do not receive their dowries. Usually it is only paid upon termination of the marriage if divorce is initiated by the husband. Taxation of the dowry reinforces a husband's financial power over his wife during marriage, and further inhibits a wife's potential for financial autonomy at the time of a divorce.

Article 46 [40] criminalizes the marriage of a foreigner to an Iranian woman without proper authorization. The foreign man is subject to between ninety days and one year's imprisonment, and the woman (if she married of her free will), her father (if he gave permission) and the marriage official will be sentenced as accomplices.

In September 2008, over 50 secular and Islamist women activist decided to prevent bill's ratification. They demanded to meet the members of parliament presenting a proposal to change the controversial provisions. [41] Ultimately, they succeeded in convincing the parliament to postpone the ratification pending further investigation. However, in January 2010, the spokesperson of law and legal affairs committee of the parliament announced that the committee has reinstated the polygamy clause with some modifications including that "a man can marry a second wife under ten conditions. The new version still requires the first wife to give permission, though controversially, this would not be required under certain condition such as if she is mentally ill, or suffers from infertility, has a chronic medical condition, or is addicted to drugs, in which case the husband can marry another woman. Also, if the first wife does not cooperate sexually, the husband can take another wife. [42]

Another provision of the bill that would encourage temporary marriage which has become more common in Iran under the conservatives was removed in 2010. The paradox here is that Ahmadinejad campaigned on the promise to strengthen family and family values. However, a bill that legalizes polygamy, "and gives a free pass to polygamists", as suggested by Shirin Ebadi in effect weakens the structure of the family. [43] For Ahmadinejad though, it is clear that strengthening the family implies strengthening the position of men. Traditional women in the parliament also argued in favour of polygamy as these women suggest that polygamous families are helpful to women in particular as wives can assist each other in their matrimonial duties and can benefit from their respective companionship. [44]

There were once again incidents of women being stoned for alleged adultery, a practice that disappeared during the reform era. A 2008 film released in Iran, Second Wife (*Zan-e Dovom*) also encouraged support for the polygamist message. Several programs on state run radio and television promote polygamy and *sigheh* and endeavour to teach women how to cope with them. [45]

4.4 Citizenship and Inheritance

According to Articles 976 and 964 of the civil law, [46] Iranian women who are married to non-Iranians cannot pass on their nationality and citizenship to their husbands and children. On the other hand, non-Iranians who are married to Iranian men automatically become Iranian nationals and citizens and can apply for an Iranian identity card and passport. In 2006, the parliament passed an amendment to the citizenship law allowing women married to foreign nationals to pass on their citizenship to their children. The new legislation permits this transfer of citizenship as long as the child in 18, the father is a Muslim and the parents have a legalized marriage. While the legal change has been applauded, activists have criticized the measure as half-hearted as children would continue to be "stateless" until the age of 18, rendering them ineligible for public benefits and social services. [47]

According to Article 946 of the Civil Code of Iran, which is based on Islamic law, the "husband inherits all the property of the deceased wife, but the wife of a deceased husband inherits only movable property of any kind and buildings and trees. The law provided a restriction on a woman's inheritance of buildings and trees by saying that the woman inherits the value of the buildings and trees, not the actual real estate. However, the law did provide that if the other survivors of the husband refuse to pay the wife the price of the real property, then the wife can acquire the real property itself". [48]

In 2009, Iranian parliament passed legislation making it possible for women to inherit up to a quarter of the land and standing property from their husbands. The previous law only allowed women to inherit a portion of the portable property prohibiting their inheritance of real estate. [49] To put it simply, this legislation has introduced the following innovations. First, land has been added to the property a woman may inherit from a deceased husband, something which was banned before; and second, limits on the proportion of movable property a woman could inherit have been deleted. Ahmadinejad issue a decree that instructs all government bodies to enforce this recently passed law, despite Guardian Council's silence over the issue.

4.5 Hejab

The government launched a political campaign, what is informally called, "culture of modesty" (*farhang-e effaf*) in 2005, which was primarily aimed at restoring the strict veiling (*hejab*) of women as practiced in the early years of the Islamic Republic and at eliminating what is called '*bad hejabi*', the women who adorned *hejab* differently than the state's prescription of wearing *hejab*. On January 3, 2006, a subsection of the Supreme Council issued a bylaw directing all ministries, government agencies and NGOs to forward the "culture of hejab and modesty". The by-law also ordered the *Basiji* [50] to challenge all manifestations of bad hejabi, with force if need be. [51] *Basiji* women were not only given the task of representing the "culture of modesty" as prescribed by the Islamic Republic of Iran but also enforced this practice upon others.

The President started the Social Morality Plan (*Tarhe Amniyat Ejtema'i*) in March 2007. The program was designed to combat immorality and criminality. The first and the most visible component of this program was a campaign addressing lax adherence to Islamic *hejab* standards. Through increased police vigilance, police have identified and detained women who fail to comply with the Islamic dress code. The police were strategically dispatched to congested locations where they could target women. The targets were detained until the family members brought them clothing deemed to be in compliance with the law. They were generally given warnings and forced to sign a commitment that obliges them to dress appropriately. Repeat offenders were referred to the judicial system where sentences included fines and even lashings. [52]

In 2006, the Centre announced a programme of "Plan of Mercy" with a budget of 10 billion Rials ($1 million) that aimed at encouraging *hejab* while confronting *bad hejab,* and promoting marriage and domestication of women and discouraging the practice of women working outside the home. *Basiji* women and students at women's seminaries were entrusted the task of implementing the government's program in the *Basij*-affiliated mosques that exist in most urban neighbourhoods and many small towns. The Women's Studies Centre of the Qom Seminary was another important think tank that was pressed by the government to counter the influence of Islamic feminism and propagate the 'virtue' of marrying at a very young age. The Seminary publishes books and periodicals and holds seminars, particularly for *Basiji* women. A third institution that was enlisted in the 'modesty campaign' was the Supreme Council of the Cultural Revolution, which works to ensure that cultural production, including university textbooks, toes the regime's line. [53]

In line with government's approach on women the Tehran mayor, Muhammad Baqir Qalibaf, established an all women park known as 'Mother's Paradise', where women were encouraged to engage in sports and exercise. However, by no means this was the only single sex park. Similar parks exclusively for women have already been opened. Developments such as these are seen by the Centre for Women and Family Affairs. Using similar outreach strategies, the government has drawn on its female *Basij* network to spread the official policy of modesty and family values throughout the country. At the same time, through such incorporative measures, these women are involved in the social and economic sustenance of the country, moves designed to empower women within the Islamic system. [54] Female only police stations were set up in Mashad, with plans to extend the design to Tehran. Female police officers were used in the government effort to crack down on those flouting Islamic dress codes and social mores.

4.6 Sports

In April 2006, President Ahmadinejad made an attempt to champion the cause of women rights by expressing his opinion in favour of lifting the ban on women attendance of men's national sports matches. Ahmadinejad's statement was released in the midst of an ongoing campaign of female soccer fans that created rumblings amongst the conservative section including ulema of Iranian political establishment. In June 2005 a group of a 100 women pushed their way into Azadi stadium in Tehran to watch the soccer match between their national team and Bahrain. The victory over Bahrain, qualifying Iran for the 2006 World Cup, sparked mass celebrations in the streets of Tehran. [55] While the authorities could hardly prevent the spontaneous patriotic outbreak, they barely tolerated the intermixed gender gatherings, and the presence of unveiled women. The high ranking *ulema* were irked, to say the least, that they had not been consulted about the reversal of the ban. The controversy came to an end only when Khamenei, the Supreme Leader, intervened to ask Ahmadinejad to retract his statements. [56]

4.7 Press and NGO's

As recently as September 2006, the Ministry of Islamic and Cultural Guidance closed down two prominent daily Iranian newspapers, *Shargh* and *Nameh.* In January 2008, feminist monthly magazine *Zanan* was banned. The grounds for closure was that it "endangered the spiritual, mental and intellectual health of its readers" promoting insecurity in society, disturbed public rights, weakened military and revolutionary institutes. It also accused of publishing articles that "led people to believe that Islamic Republic is unsafe for women". [57] This closure was notable in the sense that *Zanan* was regarded as a monthly magazine that cautiously avoided politics and focuses exclusively on women's issues. *Zanan*'s closure, coming a few months prior to the *Majles* election held in March 2008 suggested a continuous campaign of repression directed at the reform movement and at the independent press. [58]

Under the reformist government and parliament, women were active in the NGO's but Ahmadinejad's government closed down many NGO's when western countries particularly, the United States, announced a policy of funding NGO's in Iran in order to bring about regime change. [59] However, this policy of funding in Iran has greatly damaged women's participation in the public domain. Most of the NGO's remaining were state sponsored. All these have made women's work more difficult as many independent ones have been closed down.

4.8 Political Participation

During Ahmadinejad's first and second presidential campaigns, there was no gesture to include women in high political and managerial positions nor was there any programme for the inclusion of women in decision-making positions. There was no indication in Ahmadinejad's manifesto about women rights issue. The emphasis was mainly on women's role in the family. However, once in office he appointed a number of women as his deputies and advisors, who in effect participated in making policies as part of his government. [60] This demonstrates that women's struggle for changes since 1990s has been effective and no political leader can ignore the interests of women.

Table 4.6 shows percentage of female candidates and MPs in the Iranian Parliament.

Table 4.7 indicates the proportionate distribution of women candidates in the Parliament.

Table 4.6: Percentage of Female Candidates and MPs in the Iranian Parliament in Comparison with the Male Candidates and MPs

Parliament	Year	Percent of Female Candidates	Percent of Female MPs
3rd	1988-1992	1.6	1.6
4th	1992-1996	3.0	3.6
5th	1996-2000	6.4	5.6
6th	2000-2004	7.3	4.4
7th	2004-2008	9.8	4.4
8th	2008-2012	8.0	2.7

Source: Koolaee, Elaheh, "Women in Parliament", 2012, in Tara Povey and Elaheh Rostami Povey (eds.), 'Women, Power and Politics in 21st Century Iran', p. 138, Ashgate Publishing Limited.

Table 4.7: Proportionate Distribution of Women Candidates in Iranian Parliament

Parliament	Number of Women Deputies
4th	9
5th	14
6th	13
7th	13
8th	8

Sources: Moinifar, Heshamat Sadat, "Participation of Women in Iran's Polity", accessed at:
http://www.law.tohoku.ac.jp/gcoe/wp-content/uploads/2011/03/gemc_04_cate2_4.pdf.

Table 4.8 shows the number of bills passed which were directly related to the status of women.

Table 4.9 shows the position of female candidates in the city council elections.

Table 4.10 indicates female candidacy for parliamentary elections.

Following the example of Khatami, Ahmadinejad in his first term included a number of women as vice presidents and advisors in his administration. Fatemeh Javadi became vice president of Department of Environment and Nasrin Soltankhah was appointed as the head of the Centre for Family and Women's Affairs. Later, Soltankhah became a member of Tehran city council and was replaced by Tabib Zadeh, who became the president's advisor on women's issues.

Table 4.8: Number of Bills Related Directly to the Status of Women, Passed by Each Parliament

Majles (Parliament)	Bills Passed by Majles
Third (1988-1992)	6
Fourth (1992-1996)	8
Fifth (1996-2000)	21
Sixth (2000-04)	17
Seventh (2004-08)	13

Sources: Moinifar, Heshamat Sadat, "Participation of Women in Iran's Polity", accessed at: http://www.law.tohoku.ac.jp/gcoe/wp-content/uploads/2011/03/gemc_04_cate2_4.pdf.

Table 4.9: Number of Female Candidates and the Number of Elected Female Councillors in the City Council Elections (1999-2006)

Year	No. of Female Candidates	No. of Elected Female Councillors
First Council Elections, 1998	7,276	1,375
Second Council Elections, 2002	5,867	2,336
Third Council Elections, 2006	7,106	1,491

Source: Nejadbahram, Zahra, "Women in Parliament", 2012, in Tara Povey and Elaheh Rostami Povey (eds.), 'Women, Power and Politics in 21st Century Iran', p. 86, Ashgate Publishing Limited.

During his second term, Nasrin Soltankhah and Fatemeh Bodaghi have been appointed as vice presidents. Soltankhah, as advisor in scientific and technological issues, became the head of the Research and Training Institute for Management and Development Planning. Bodaghi became the legal advisor to the head of Iran's judiciary.

Table 4.10: Female Candidacy for Parliamentary Elections

Year	Number of Female Candidates	Total Candidates	Women as Percent of Total Candidates
1992-1996	81	3223	2.51
1996-2000	320	5366	5.96
2000-2004	513	6853	7.49
2004-2008	829	4679	5.64
2008-2012	585	7168	12.2

Source: Vakil, Sanam (2012), "Women and Politics in the Islamic Republic of Iran: Action and Reaction", p. 125, Bloomsbury Academic.

Maryam Mojtahedzadeh replaced Tabib Zadeh as the advisor on women's and family affairs and Soosan Keshavarz became an advisor on education. In 2009, he proposed three women, viz. Marzieh Vahid Dastjerdi, Fatemeh Ajorloo and Soosan Keshavarz as the ministers of health, social welfare and education, respectively and stated:

"It is important to have women in the cabinet; it is for the first time after the 1979 revolution that three committed women have been proposed to occupy ministerial position. This is an important issue as we have to acknowledge the rightful demands of our society. The presence of women in the cabinet contributes to confidence building among women in our country. They can be role models for our young women...The Ministries of Education, Health and Social Welfare are important institutions. Women have the main responsibility for education and social welfare. Women's health is also important as women could suffer from more diseases and healthier mothers, women and girls create a healthier society. For this reason, we propose three committed

women for these ministerial positions. Having women in the cabinet is most significant cultural act for country and will take the message of Iranian revolution to the world...some may be unhappy about women in these positions...they must be assured that what we do not want to draw a distinction between men and women. We see them as being complimentary to one another". [61]

This marked a new era in Iran. Though women have been playing an important role in the public sphere but no woman was appointed directly as a cabinet minister in post-revolution until 2009. However, his nomination of three women for top ministerial position was interpreted by the critics as a ploy to compensate for any perceived legitimacy deficit caused by the controversial 2009 presidential elections. [62] The Ahmadinejad government faced severe criticism for its nominations of three females as cabinet ministers from high ranking Ayatollahs in Qom to conservative parliamentarians. Ahmadinejad's female nominees provoked significant debates. [63] Out of the three women, only one was approved by the *Majles*. The two other woman nominees were rejected, due to "lack of experience". [64]

Further the government of Ahmadinejad also claimed that women could stand for local and regional elections and that in some provinces women would be appointed as governors. [65] It appears that this unexpected political gesture towards women's representation in power structures, which also provoked the conservative *Ulema*, was not guided by a genuine political will and desire on the part of Ahmadinejad regime but was in part a response of his government to the mass participation of women in the demonstrations which followed the election as well as an answer to the reformist challenges.

The absence of reformist desire and political will on the part of Ahmadinejad administration is evident from the selection of women who were elected to the seventh parliament. During the seventh parliament, the conservatives formed the majority with 54 percent of the seats while reformers were in minority with 13 percent. As a result, in this parliament all female MPs were conservative with the exception of one reformist, Mehrangiz Morovati. In isolation, she found it difficult to push for reform of the laws and regulations in favour of women. In this Parliament, the Women's Fractions, which had been formed in the sixth parliament, has been dissolved. The majority of women MPs in the seventh parliament belonged to *Basiji* (Mobilisation) who campaigned and voted for Ahmadinejad. They had a very different approach to women's roles and duties, women's rights issues were not their priority.

During the sixth parliament, in the process of amending the Fourth Development Plan, the reformist female MPs changed the term gender equality to gender justice, so that the term would be compatible with the religious and traditional perceptions of society. However, the seventh parliament ignored this concept and the new female MPs did not challenge male MPs for ignoring women's issues.

In the Fourth Development Plan, under the reformist the emphasis was to create equal opportunities for men and women, to highlight the stability and sustainability of family life but not at the expense of women's participation in public domain. But after the coming of conservatives, they tried to limit the opportunities for women and created restrictions in social activities. Moreover, the female MPs did not pay attention to the women's issues. Female MPs argued that priority of women should be their reproductive duties within the home, thus, they proposed to reduce women's working hours so that they can spend more time at home. Female MPs only focused on enforcing Islamic dress codes. There had been very little room in this Parliament for women on various boards of the parliament and on parliamentary commissions and committees. [66] In addition, there were repeated crackdowns, arrests of women's rights activists. On 8 March, 2007, International Women's Day, Iranian women were prevented from standing in solidarity with their female counterparts worldwide in recognition of women's rights. Women activists were government targets as more and more women have received prison sentences for their participation in One Million Signatures Campaign. [67]

Endnotes

1. Akbari, Azadeh, "The Women's Movement: An Emerging Power", available at: http://www.lse.ac.uk/IDEAS/publications/reports/pdf/SU002/akbari.pdf.
2. Moinifar, Heshamat Sadat, "Participation of Women in Iran's Polity", available at: http://www.law.tohoku.ac.jp/gcoe/wp-content/uploads/2011/03/gemc_04_cate2_4.pdf.
3. Sadeghi, Fatemeh (2009), "Foot Soldiers of the Islamic Republic's Culture of Modesty", Middle East Report No. 250, The Islamic Revolution at 30, Spring, p. 52.
4. Ibid.
5. Vakil, Sanam (2012), "Women and Politics in the Islamic Republic of Iran: Action and Reaction", p. 185, Bloomsbury Academic.
6. For details, see Akbari, No. 1.
7. Shahrokni, Nazanin (2009), "All the President's Women", Middle East Report No. 253, Winter, p. 3.
8. Esfandiari, Haleh, "For Women of the Arab Spring: Iranian Women Provide a Warning and a Model", available at: http://www.turkishpolicy.com/dosyalar/files/vol_11-no_4 percent20esfandiari.pdf.
9. Rezai-Rashti, Goli M., "The Future of Iran: Educational Reform Women and Education in the Islamic Republic of Iran: Repressive Policies, Unexpected Outcomes", p. 7, accessed at: http://www.li.com/docs/default-source/default-document-library/women-and-education-in-the-islamic-republic-of-iran-repressive-policies-unexpected-outcomes.
10. Nejadbahram, Zahra, "Women and Employment", in Tara Povey and Elaheh Rostami Povey (eds.), 'Women, Power and Politics in 21st Century Iran", p. 79, Ashgate Publishing Limited.
11. Vakil, No. 5, p. 189.
12. See Akbari, No. 1.

13. For the above data, see Rezai-Rashti, Goli M., No. 9, p. 7.
14. Vakil, No. 5, p. 189.
15. Rezai-Rashti, Goli M., No. 9, p. 7.
16. Aryan, Khadijeh, "The Boom in Women's Education", 2012, in Tara Povey and Elaheh Rostami Povey (eds.), 'Women, Power and Politics in 21st Century Iran', p. 47, Ashgate Publishing Limited.
17. Concour (competition) is a centralized test to gain admission to higher education in Iran. The Ministry of Higher Education standardize the system and today the examination consists of general and specialized multiple choice questions. Students are accepted into universities on the basis of marks they obtain in this examination.
18. Mehran, Golnar, "Doing and Undoing Gender: Female Higher Education in the Islamic Republic of Iran", p. 543, available at: http://www.jstor.org/stable/40608077.
19. Ibid., p. 550.
20. Aryan, No. 16, p. 47.
21. Ibid., p. 37.
22. Rezai-Rashti, Goli M., No. 9, p. 7.
23. For the facts in the above paragraph see Vakil, No. 5, p. 185.
24. Cincotta, Richard, "Prospects for Ahmadinejad's Call for More Rapid Population Growth in Iran", available at: http://www.stimson.org/summaries/prospects-for-ahmadinejads-call-for-more-rapid-population-growth-in-iran.
25. Baavur, Liora Hendelman, "A Mid-Term Assessment of Ahmadinejad's Gender Policy", available at: http://www.aftau.org/site/DocServer/iran_pulse_16.pdf.pdf?docID=2341.
26. Barlow, Rebecca and Akbarzadeh, Shahram (2008), "Prospects for Feminism in the Islamic Republic of Iran", *Human Rights Quarterly,* Vol. 30, No. 1, February, p. 22.
27. For the above facts, see Afary, Janet (2009), "Sexual Politics in Iran", p. 350, Cambridge University Press.
28. For the above data, see "Iran's Leader Introduces Plan to Encourage Population Growth by Paying Families", available at: http://www.nytimes.com/2010/07/28/world/middleeast/28iran.html.
29. Nejadbahram, No. 10, p. 79.
30. Aryan, No. 16, p. 49.

31. Ibid., p. 49.
32. Nejadbahram, No. 10, p. 84.
33. Ibid., p. 78.
34. For the data in the above paragraph, see Moghadam, Valentine M., "Where Are Iran's Working Women"?, available at: http://www.mei.edu/content/where-are-irans-working-women.
35. Nejadbahram, No. 10, p. 81.
36. Ibid., p. 76.
37. Kian, Azadeh, "Gendered Citizenship and the Women's Movement in Iran", in Parsi, Rouzbeh (ed.), 'Iran: A Revolutionary Republic in Transition', p. 67, available at: http://www.ab.gov.tr/files/ardb/evt/1_avrupa_birligi/1_9_politikalar/1_9_8_dis_politika/Iran_A_revolutionary_republic_in_transition.pdf.
38. Ibid., p. 67.
39. Ibid.
40. Ibid.
41. Ibid., p. 68.
42. Vakil, No. 5, p. 188.
43. Ibid.
44. Ibid.
45. Sadeghi, No. 3, p. 52.
46. Koolaee, Elaheh (2012), "Women in Parliament", in Tara Povey and Elaheh Rostami Povey (eds.), 'Women, Power and Politics in 21st Century Iran', p. 147, Ashgate Publishing Limited.
47. Vakil, No. 5, p. 186.
48. The data and facts in the above paragraph have been taken from Vafai, Gholam, "Iran: New Women's Inheritance Law is Enforced", available at: http://www.loc.gov/lawweb/servlet/lloc_news?disp3_l205401290.
49. Vakil, No. 5, p. 186.
50. Basij (Mobilisation) is a paramilitary volunteer militia founded after the 1979 revolution that was originally called "The Mobilisation of the Oppressed" or "The Mobilisation Resistance Force". In more recent years, the Basij serves as an auxiliary force in internal security and law enforcement.
51. For the data in the above paragraph, see Sadeghi, No. 3, pp. 52-54.
52. For the data, see Vakil, No. 5, p. 187.

53. The data in the above paragraph has been taken from Sadeghi, No. 3, p. 53.
54. For the data, see Vakil, No. 5, p. 190.
55. Baavur, No. 25.
56. Shahrokni, No. 7, p. 3.
57. Vakil, No. 5, p. 189.
58. Ibid.
59. Koolaee, No. 46, p. 148.
60. For the data see Kadivar, Jamileh, "Women and Executive Power", 2012, in Tara Povey and Elaheh Rostami Povey (eds.), 'Women, Power and Politics in 21st Century Iran', p. 125, Ashgate Publishing Limited.
61. Kadivar, No. 60, p. 127.
62. Ibid.
63. Ibid., pp.127-128.
64. Shahrokni, No. 7, p. 3.
65. Ibid., p. 132.
66. For the facts and data in the above two paragraphs, see Koolaee, No. 46, pp. 144-145.
67. Vakil, No. 5, p. 191.

5

Women's Movements in Iran: Nature, Discourses and Responses

From the preceding chapters what emerges is that the state and the regimes have constructed different narratives of gender in order to signify particular identity of state and government. Ayatollah Khomeini constructed the more conservative Islamic discourse about gender relationship, role of gender in the construction of national identity and overall subordinate position of women in the Iranian society. The same discourse was returned in Iran during Ahmadinejad period. On the other hand, the Rafsanjani and Khatami regime constructed a more liberal, reformist discourse of gender relationship in order to differentiate from Khomeini regime as well as to end the isolation of Iran in the international system.

The gender discourse from Khomeini to Ahmadinejad was also shaped by the responses from the plethora of women's organizations/groups—both secular and Islamic—that kept emerging and existed in formal, discrete and informal ways since the inception of Islamic revolution. This chapter focuses on the nature, discourses and responses of various women's agencies/groups/organizations as well as their strategies and pattern of mobilization and negotiation with the government that sometimes resulted in the empowerment of women rights and sometimes in de-empowerment. The trend of 'contraction and expansion' of women rights as a result of struggle and negotiation between various women organization and various governments of the day has existed and continue to exist throughout the period ranging from Khomeini to Ahmadinejad.

Before analyzing the nature, discourses and responses of the various women organizations to the specific public policies of the various government initiated from time to time and its outcome in

Post Khomeini period, it is important to briefly sketch out the late Imam Khomeini's policies towards women as well as the latter's responses in order to discern the continuity and changes in women's activism in post Khomeini period.

5.1 Women's Movement during Khomeini Period

As the Islamic Republic under Khomeini consolidated its power and position it quickly moved to embark on the policy of Islamisation of Iranian society. Women became the most visible target of this Islamisation policy as a marker of Islamic nation. Soon they were confronted with having no choice but to live an 'Islamic life' as prescribed by the Islamic regime as evident from scrapping the Family Protection Law, barring women from becoming judges, making hejab compulsory at least at the workplace and later for women in all public places, segregating the beaches and sports as well as the educational choices the details of which have been listed in the preceding chapter. [1]

The unexpected turn of events resulted in spontaneous demonstrations which continued for several weeks. Moreover these developments brought into focus a small gathering organized for March 8, International Women's Day, by a small group of women with leftist tendencies. The massive demonstrations of March 1979 included urban women of all social backgrounds. This event, which normally would go unnoticed, grew into a protest rally, as thousands demonstrated against the undemocratic imposition of these codes. [2] Women lawyers, backed by secular as well as some Islamist forces, organized several sit-ins in the Ministry of Justice. [3] Despite a boycott of protest rallies by the media, including the national radio and television, the demonstrations attracted public attention and support. The media estimated that 20,000 women participated in that protest rally, and many more joined the march which followed it. [4]

The political protest and ferment led to mushrooming of women organisations. Earlier during the years 1978-79, the

Women's Organization of Iran that was associated with Pahlavi regime was abolished, but several new ones were established, and some old ones re-emerged. These included the National Union of Women, the Committee for Solidarity of Women, the Organization of Iranian Women, Women's Populace of Iran, Women's branch of National Democratic Front, the Association of Women Lawyers, the Women's Society of Islamic Revolution, and the Muslim Women's Movement. The latter two, [5] along with a number of small but influential other associations affiliated with the Islamic Republic Party and other Islamic charities, represented Muslim women loyal to the Islamic revolution and the newly established Islamic Republic.

5.2 Nature of Resistance by Secular Women Organisations

Secular women activists tried to organize independent women's organizations such as National Union of Women and Women's Emancipation to fight against these developments. Some of the organizations, supported by experienced and educated members, became vocal critics of the provisional government. Others attempted to reach grassroots women and build awareness, initiating training and literacy classes. This burst of organized secular feminist activity, however, was short-lived. The Islamic government used the Iran-Iraq war and threats of infiltration by pro-Shah forces as opportunities to crush organized political groups. Women's organizations were high on their agenda, and many of their active members were arrested and jailed. Others, faced with this repressive situation, went into exile where many continued to write and be active on the question of women. [6]

However, the suppression of secular parties has meant that for all practical purposes, only religious parties, or those willing to pay lip service to Islam by adding a religious adjective to their name, could function. [7] Many women activists who remained in the country re-emerged by the mid and late 1980s, forming small, informal consciousness-raising or training groups, while others continued to write.

5.3 Emergence of Islamic Women Movement

It was under such political context that Islamic women movement—partly supported by the government and partly self formed—emerged at the Iranian national political scene. Gradually, organizations that pledged loyalty to the IRI managed to obtain approval from the Interior Ministry. The process of registration began in mid 1980s and continued since then. The largest number of registration of women organisations took place during Rafsanjani and Khatami period. As per 2009 Report, there were some 240 registered political organizations, 18 of which were women's organizations. [8] Many of these organizations do not fit the conventional political party models, rather they are more like political and professional associations with a particular political program and perspectives. Many of these women organisations are registered under the Ministry of Interior's Political Parties Act which gives them a wider scope of activism than allowed under other Acts on rights of assembly. [9]

Khomeini's strategy for supplanting the secular feminist-oriented women's organization with Islamic women's organizations created the opportunity for women to become involved in the discourse of post-revolutionary gender ideology. *The regime projected an image of the ideal Iranian women as "exalted Muslims...both guardians of the family and active public agents.*" [10] This image was inspired largely by the writings of Ali Shariati and Morteza Motahari, whose constructions of the model Muslim woman were based on personages of the Prophet's daughter, Fatemeh and his grand-daughter Zeinab who, according to them, were simultaneously "true home makers and public persons". [11] This "women in the family" social framework posited that by virtue of their biological differences, men and women were better suited for different social roles.

This model was adopted by the Women's Society of the Islamic Revolution (WSIR) which was formed soon after the revolution. The prominent woman associated with WSIR included, among others, Zahra Mostafavi (Khomeini's daughter), Azam Taleghani, Fereshteh Hashemi, Shahin Tabatabai and Shahla Habibi, most of whom were members of prominent clerical families and who advocated the complementary nature of men and women. The WSIR was the new state-sponsored women's organization that worked to influence and organize women in favour of an 'authentic' Islamic identity for Iranian women, as well as to garner support for the government itself. *Working within the vision of Islamic revolution WSIR emphasized on the "family [as] the heart of the society, and women the heart of family".* [12] Furthermore, these Islamic women contended that within the confines of "an Islamic state led by *velayat-e faqih*, there would be no need for special organizations to defend women's rights". [13]

Most of its members were educated in the West. Fereshteh Hashemi, Shahin Tabatabai and Zahra Rahnavard; all held doctorates from American universities. Others were connected to respected religious leaders or had made a name for themselves as a result of their political activities against the Pahlavi regime. [14] Azam Taleghani (daughter of Ayatollah Taleghani) who was elected to the *Majles* was a co-founder of society. She also founded *Payam-e Hajer,* a woman's newspaper, which was dedicated to promulgating a view of women approved by the leaders of the Islamic Republic. [15] Fatemah Hashemi (daughter of Ali Akbar Hashemi Rafsanjani, president of the Islamic Republic) became the head of the Women's Bureau of the Ministry of Foreign Affairs and the Women's Solidarity Association of Iran. [16] Thus, by setting up WSIR and other women's organizations, these women began an unprecedented Islamic reformist women movement. The movement set out to create a vision of the ideal Islamic society and the role of women in it.

The organization provided services for poor women, including legal and psychological counselling, but viewed its contributions to public discourse and the advancement of women's concerns as its most important role. Taleghani frequently stated that there can be no Islamic justice without gender justice. [17] The organization published the journal *Payam-e Hajer* for two decades, including critical reports on polygamy, family law and the lack of democracy. The organization continues to push for women's legal equity. In fact, Taleghani was the first woman to formally talk about CEDAW and the need for its ratification by the Islamic Republic. [18] The organization was from its early years also a training ground for many emerging women activists who went on to other arenas.

In addition to WSIR, another prominent Islamic reformist women organisation is the Zeinab Society *(Jameh Zeinab)*, founded by anti-Shah activists, many of whom received theological education in Qom. Many founding members were previously part of the National Islamic Republican Party, established immediately after the Revolution and subsequently closed down by Khomeini in 1987 ostensibly to prevent a national political schism. The Zeinab Society has branches in two provincial centres, 60 towns, and 22 areas of Tehran. The organization oversees eight women's *Houzeh Elmieh* (seminaries) in Qom and some Qur'anic centres. [19] It is based on the principle that Islam sanctions an equality of men and women, and that the injustices that women are subject to are the result of a patriarchal reading of Islamic texts. [20]

Thus, they attempt to address gender inequalities from within the Islamic framework. According to their constitution, only women who are committed to the principles of Islam, the Islamic revolution, and *Velayat-e Faqih* can join the organization. All members must participate in training workshops and be active in the political, cultural and religious life of their communities while working to bring about change. *The Society's motto is a quotation from Ayatollah Khomeini: "Women should not assume that they can sit home and let men do the work. Everyone, wherever he/she is, should work to improve his/her community".* It was also the first women's political organization to formally introduce the idea of a female quota for elected offices in post-revolutionary Iran. [21]

There are several other established Reformist women's political organizations whose founders had strong family or marriage ties to influential religious-political leaders. Farida Mostafavi, daughter of Ayatollah Khomeini, and her associates set up the Society of Islamic Revolutionary Women in 1986, though they began activities several years earlier. Their mandate is to remove every type of discrimination against women, improve women's position within the family, promote the presence of women at all top decision-making levels, promote women's well-being at all levels, and promote contact and communication within and outside the country among women's organizations. They have consistently put forward candidates for national elections and published the magazine, *Neda*, whose public position is rather conservative. [22] Their activities have diminished in the post-Khatami period.

5.4 Emergence of Critical Islamic Women's Voices

Islamist reformist women expected not only that the new government would work with them, providing financial support and making it possible for them to continue with their mission, but also that they would be invited by the government to participate in policy making and consult on gender issues. [23] However to their disillusionment, none of these expectations materialized. These women, despite their commitment to Islam, saw the regime's policies as misguided and repressive—the old patriarchal system in new clothes. The true Islam they envisioned was woman-friendly and gender balanced. In contrast to the regime, they spoke not of the glorious past but rather of a glorious future, to be realized if a more woman-centered understanding of Islam were pursued. [24] Gradually they became more vocal by the end of 1980s airing their grievances through the strategy of 'power of presence' [25] and re-interpretation of Islamic text that made the political context and national public opinion more receptive to their demands and grievances.

Thus, women began to engage the religious establishment with '*female-centered interpretations of Islam*', becoming innovators in developing an 'Islamic feminist theory of women's oppression and liberation'. [26] Many Islamist women, who were well versed in religious matters, presented a new gender vision based on a woman-cantered interpretation of Islamic text. They pointed out that much of what is being presented to women as Islamic and 'authentic Islamic ways' is nothing but 'patriarchy in Islamic costume'. [27]

Open criticisms like these put Islamist women activists in disfavour with the regime. Since WSIR and Zeinab society was articulating their position within the term of reference of Islam and its leaders were associated with the Islamic revolution and retains its Islamic legitimacy it was not possible for the regime to deal with them in coercive manner as they did with secular oriented women organizations. The regime instead prefers a 'replacement strategy' [28] which was easier to carry out as WSIR was more or less a state organization. Thus, the more conservative faction of the state manipulated the WSIR activities by driving out the reformist women and put its own supporters in control to make it possible to mobilize women for the state initiated programmes.

Women like Azam Taleghani and Fereshteh Hashemi who had been associated with the deposed President Bani Sadr were forced into silence. Zahra Rahnavard who introduced herself as a 'follower of the party of God, but not belonging to any earthly party' was also intimidated into silence. [29] Similarly the Islamic Republican Party also managed to replace outspoken Islamist women on the *Zan-e Ruz* editorial board with their own supporters. [30] Another popular radical Islamist women's magazine, *Rah-e Zeinab* (which like *Zan-Ruz* existed before the revolution but was renamed), was forced to close. [31]

However, a second category of religious women, being

critical of the leader's conservative vision, were willing to work within the regime's framework, hoping to achieve gradual shift in the government's position on women. While continuing to reaffirm their commitment to the Islamic Republic at every opportunity, they also warned against the excesses of the Republic's gender ideology and its incompatibility with existing social realities. Knowing there were few sympathetic ears among the leaders, these women activists took their case to the public, using whatever modern and traditional institutions were open to them.

At the same time many supporters of the women's rights continued to write for women's magazines in a milder and more acceptable tone, nonetheless revealing the contradiction of trying to build a just Islamic society primarily through exposing women to unjust hardship, both within the family and society in the name of Islam. By doing this, they continued to raise awareness. This strategy was so successful that a new magazine, *Khanvadeh* (Family), was launched primarily to feature family problems. [32]

As the magazine never claimed to be a woman's magazine, it was read by both men and women, it became primarily a forum for women to gain support for complaints and legal problems concerning marriage, divorce, custody of their children etc. Magazines such as *Zan-e Ruz* [33] were also filled with individual tales of hardships, humiliation and suffering of women under male dominated legal and social contracts. These magazines became the subject of women's discussions and even local religious leaders felt obliged to address some of the issues or specific cases in their sermons.

Thus, through this slowly, gradual, peaceful process section of both men and women took the gender issues directly to the public through print media, women's religious gatherings, and sometimes via radio and television. They exposed the injustices suffered by women in the name of creating a 'just' Islamic society, and invited the public to be the judge. [34] As a result least some members of the political-religious leadership began searching for a solution.

Another manifestation of the success of women's campaign introduction of a new marriage contract which was devised to help women in order to have some control over the kind of marriage they entered into. [35] The marriage contract spelled out those infringements of women's rights which could give them the right to initiate divorce. Some of the grounds upon which women can initiate divorce were: husband's refusal to pay *nafagheh*, husband's long-term illness or insanity, his employment in jobs demeaning to her and her family, husband's imprisonment for over five years, addiction, unreasonable absence from home for over six months, the husband's infertility or impotence and his marriage to another woman without her consent. In 1989, the *Majles* passed the Divorce Reform Bill, which though left a man's unilateral divorce rights unchanged, but required a court's permission before the divorce could be registered.

This success was followed by a decree from Ayatollah Khomeini granting martyr's widows custody of their children even after remarriage. While this law does not extend to all women, its significance stems from breaking with the *Shi'i* belief that custody laws are *Qur'anic* and not subject to challenge. Similarly Iranian women campaigned for the *ojrat ol-mesal* (wages for housework) during Khomeini period also succeeded in getting the law passed in December 1991 that finally became an Act in 1992 despite opposition. Islamic women activists argued that women, like all other Muslims, are entitled to the fruit of their labour on the grounds that Islam is against exploitation, but that for centuries women have been denied this basic right. One advantage of this law is that if a man who intends to divorce his wife without proving fault on her part must first pay housework wages for the duration of the marriage. Many women feel that, despite its problematic application, this law has provided a better bargaining position than ever before. [36]

Criticism of government performance from women

activists also resulted in the establishment of the Social and Cultural Council of Women to promote women's economic and social activity. In 1992 the Office of Women's Affairs, an offshoot of the Presidential Bureau, was created to identify specific women related problems and shortcomings and to propose solutions to uplift social, political and economic status and role of women in the Iranian society.

5.5 Weakness of Women's Movement

There were number of factors that obstructed the women's movements to realize its goals during Khomeini period. Some of these factors continue to work at present also and therefore will be referred while discussing the issues of women's movement in post Khomeini period. The first factor that obstructed the goals of women movements was the national context of Iran-Iraq War and the US hostile attitude against Iran that had began immediately after the revolution. Both these factors allowed the regime to mobilize the national opinion and voices including the women organisations defend the Iranian nation against the perceived threat of imperialism against the Iranian revolution.

Second, the failure of the women's movement was partly due to weak organizational structure and lack of adequate sociological features of social movement. *Highlighting this aspect of failure of women's movement in Iran, Mahdi opined, "in its pre-revolutionary stage, the Iranian women's movement never developed the sociological characteristics necessary for a successful social movement—characteristics such as a well-defined set of objectives, planned regular activities, adequate organizational structures and networks, a stable and/or organized cadre of activists, a leadership, a widespread membership with a "we-consciousness," a set of cohesive guiding values or ideology (identity), and clear normative expectations for social change*". [37]

Third, the women's movement was mostly located in the urban centres and led by urban educated women, who lacked the organic relationship with wider segment of women in the Iranian society and thus could not forge the solidarity network with majority of religious Iranian women living in the periphery. The urban and 'high culture' lifestyle of these women continued to differ sharply from those women of lower and traditional classes, thus making it harder to create a critical mass in support of the movement. The strategies adopted by them also had an urban bias. Women activists often published pamphlets and magazines that were not accessible to the large number of illiterate women in rural areas. These urban cantered women organisations existed only on the paper and lacked adequate resources, political will and autonomy to pressurize the government.

Fourth, the state countered the emergence of an independent women's movement in two ways: on the one hand, it did not tolerate any independent movement and continued to suppress autonomous activities capable of challenging its monopoly of power. Women's demands for independent action were perceived as a political challenge to the state and a provocative issue evoking religious opposition. On the other hand, the Islamic state, much like the Shah's state, saw itself as the 'champion' of women's rights and was a major source of social change in the status of women in the country. [38] It extended state power over women's bodies and could not tolerate changes arising outside of its own control. This, in fact, complicated the task of most 'Islamic feminists' supporting women's rights during the Khomeini era.

Lastly, the most significant aspect of the failure of the women movement was its dependence on the government or general political movements [39] that prevented the movement from developing its own unique identity, especially during 1978-81 periods. In these periods, which were characterized by an increase in the number and activities of women's organizations, women's activities were organizationally too dependent on various political parties dominated by male politicians—a condition that put women in supporting roles in those organizations. As Tabari [40] mentions, many of the women's organizations during the early years of the revolution acted as fronts for recruiting female members for the parent organizations. It is only in post-revolutionary Iran that one begins to see the re-birth of women's movement with a new identity and higher degree of autonomy.

5.6 Women's Movements in Post Khomeini Period

The large numbers of Iranian women, many of them who voluntary participated in the revolution, soon began to discover the discrepancy and contradictions between their aspirations and expectation of a dignified life in post-revolution period and actual laws that were promulgated by the Islamic regime with an intention to deprive and curtail the women rights in the name of constructing an Islamic state. It was this visual, palpable contradictions and dichotomy between the aspirations of women and a post-revolutionary thrust to institutionalize gender inequality that provided the material context to mobilize a significant numbers of Iranian women cutting across class and ideological divide against the unequal gender laws of post revolutionary Islamic state.

A number of factors contributed to undermine the Islamic Republic's project for women, family, and gender relations in the second decade of the Islamic revolution. The first factor was the death of Ayatollah Khomeini in 1989, since his death no leader has emerged as charismatic and commanded national loyalty and were therefore vulnerable to the 'politics of regime survival' that requires a fair amount of flexibility and pragmatism. A second set of factors that undermined IRI policies on women were brought about by the long war with Iraq (1980-88). The mobilization of all Iranian men created employment opportunities for educated women in the public sector, particularly in health, education, and to a lesser extent in public administration.

Though these jobs went to ideologically-correct women, but the very 'presence of women' in the public workforce suggested both the determination of women and the flexibility of the regime. Other factors affecting the IRI's Islamization policies were declining government revenues, indebtedness due to the war with Iraq, and increasing unemployment and poverty. A third set of factors was the issue of reintegration of Iran into international community. Both Rafsanjani and Khatami regimes paid special attention to end the international isolation of Iran and rebuild war torn economy which in turn demanded a more liberal state's policy towards women, along with others, to attract the foreign investment.

It was this political context that allowed the emergence of Rafsanjani and Khatami brand of liberal Islamic politics within which Islamic as well as secular movement flourished and gained new ground. In fact most of 18 registered Islamic women organisations were registered during these periods. [41] For secular activists the loss of public space has been significant since the establishment of the Islamic Republic; the public pursuit of justice from a human rights position has been almost impossible under the Islamic regime.

While some secularist women activists had left the country, the majority had continued its activities through informal gatherings, usually in their homes, and had tried to strengthen networks with Iranian expatriates and the transnational women's movement. Their Strategies included documenting the worst of the many women's human rights abuses, such as stoning and public lashing, and publicizing them internationally to create pressure on the government, as well as documenting the dismal situation of women in the family court system, publishing the stories in women's and other magazines. [42] Without direct channels of communication with the government, which in any case remained hostile, they continued to try and direct information and debate to the general public and to Islamist women. This has contributed greatly to influencing the demands of Islamist women towards a rights-based approach to the democratization of gender in Islamic discourse and Iran's legal system. [43]

5.7 Inclusion and Expansion of Women's Rights under Rafsanjani and Khatami

Rafsanjani's liberal government (1989-1997), eager to reconcile with the international community, eased restrictions somewhat leaving more opportunity for secular women to publish their writings. To refute the image of Iran as a dictatorial theocracy, the Rafsanjani government was supportive of service-oriented NGOs, which operated primarily under the leadership of wives and daughters of officials, though secular women also managed to set up some, albeit 'non-feminist', organizations. He further allowed women to represent he decided to allow women to represent Iran in various international conferences, particularly those organized under the UN umbrella. Thus, several non-governmental organizations were set up, mostly under the patronage of wives and daughters of high government officials and they subsequently participated in international meetings, including the UN Conference on Population and Development in Cairo (1994) and the Fourth World Conference on Women in Beijing (1995). Although they were controlled and repeated the government line, these experiences were eye-openers and sowed the seeds for links with the global women's movement. [44]

Under Khatami's Reformist government (1997-2005) due expansion of civil society and public participation, many secular women began writing more openly for Islamist women's magazines, engendering more direct communication and collaboration between ideologically diverse women. Websites and blogs set up by younger activists promoted legal reforms. It was during this period that Shirin Ebadi received the Nobel Peace Prize for her promotion of democracy and women's and children's rights. She brought recognition and energy to the Iranian women's movement as a whole, but especially to the secular women's movement, which was now firmly a force to reckon with. In fact, in June 2005, secular women collaboratively organized the largest oppositional protest since the early years of the Revolution, demanding an end to legal discrimination against woman and revision of the constitution. [45]

5.8 Emergence of Liberal Islamic Feminism

However, it was the liberal faction of Islamic women movement that dominated national political scene in their responses to the government policies. In fact by the early-1990s, even those women who had once subscribed to the notions of complementarity of rights at the time of the revolution began to seriously challenge them by arguing that there is no inherent or logical link between patriarchy and Islamic ideals. [46] Thus, with a shift in the discourse many of these women activists came around the idea of working within the existing political structure so as to mobilize a section of progressive *ulema* and put pressure on the government either to reverse or reform various legislations and practices that appeared discriminatory to women in general. In other words, they adopted the strategy of focusing on one issue at a time instead of many, lobbying within the political structure and especially with religious leaders and framing their demands within the Islamic traditions.

These groups of women's rights activists and their interactions and negotiations with reformist and liberal minded ulema gave rise to, 'new religious thought' (*now-andishi-ye dini*), which sought to bridge the gap between religious and secular intellectuals by adopting a pragmatic and flexible approach towards religious doctrines on democracy, freedom and human rights'. [47] The central argument of new religious thinkers was *'human understanding of Islam is flexible, in that Islam's tenets can be interpreted to encourage pluralism and democracy, and that Islam allows change in the face of time, space, and experience*'. [48]

In other words, a kind of activism emerged in Iran which argues that women's rights are indeed compatible with Islam and that what is needed is not a change in religion, but rather a change in interpretation or *ijtihad.* This new approach to feminism has been largely inspired and influenced by the work of Abdolkarim Soroush and other such as Mohsen Kadivar, Akbar Ganji, Mohsen Saidzadeh. *Saidzadeh want "to reconcile Islam with the discourse of human rights, democracy, and gender equality through what is called 'dynamic jurisprudence'.* [49] Most significantly, these intellectuals have argued that *Shari'a* should be time and place sensitive and that the provisions advocated by the Islamic Republic were largely written for a different time, place, and social context.

For the many women coming from religious background, this (*now- andishi-ye dini*) proved to be a very important tool in their fights against the patriarchal norms. Islamist women seized upon this open environment to lobby for change from within. Secular women alternatively subscribed for revisionism in order to regain lost momentum in championing female rights and equality. While there are instances of reformist and women-friendly re-interpretations of religious texts throughout Islam's history, Iranian women activists fused their religiously inspired demands with the modernist discourses of social justice and human rights. [50] In this regard, the re-interpreters emphasize a number of instances of early Muslim women who were active in some way in the public sphere, or the *Qur'anic* verses that establish gender equality.

Women's journals, such as *Zanan* (women), *Kian*, *Zan-e Ruz, Farzaneh* and *Payam-e Hajar* (*Hajar's* message), provided these intellectuals with a platform to publicize their stands on gender roles and women's rights, including women's access to key political decision-making positions, an issue which become a central demand of the Iranian women's movement. The main strategy of these groups was to publicize the contradictory views of the religious authorities on the question of status of women in Iranian Islamic society in women's magazines and other media outlets in order to make ulema accountable to their earlier promises of Islamic justice and to demonstrate the pluralities of views that exist among *ulema* with a view to extract political concession from them in the interest of women rights.

5.9 Women's Movements: Recounting of Achievements

As a result of change in the strategy of women organisations and individual women personalities, change in the political context in post-Khomeini period as well as reformist and liberal public policies of Rafsanjani and Khatami—restrictive barriers to women's mobility, educational, employment opportunities were removed as detailed in preceding chapters. However, a brief mention of them is required in order to indicate the continuity and change in the women's movement from Khomeini to post Khomeini Iran.

In 1992, the High Council of the Cultural Revolution adopted a set of Employment Policies for Women, which, while reiterating the importance of family roles and continuing to rule out certain occupations and professions as islamically inappropriate, encouraged the integration of women into the labour force and attention to their interests and needs. Women were encouraged to enter gynaecology, pharmacology, midwifery, and laboratory work. The government also opened the field of law to women in the 1990s. Women legal consultants were permitted in the Special Civil Courts, although women still could not serve as judges. About 35 percent of public sector employees today are women. Most work in the Ministries of Education and Health and about 35 percent have university degrees. [51]

Women's achievements in education have surpassed men's on many levels and in many positions. In the first decade of the revolution, enrolment in girl's primary schools had a 50 percent increase. Today, 70 percent of girls of 15-18 years age are attending high schools. In 1998, 51 percent, and in 1999, 57 percent of students entering universities were females (only 25 percent prior to the revolution) In 2000, half of all Iranian university students were women, as were 60 percent of entering students, who were selected on the basis of a difficult nationwide exam. In 2003, women's share of bachelor's degrees was nearly 50 percent, of master's degrees was 27 percent, and of Ph.D. degrees was 24 percent. [52] In the social arena, women have had the biggest gains by becoming active in the entertainment industry, journalism, and literary fields. A lively women's press emerged, with books, magazines, and women's studies journals taking on important political, cultural, religious, and social issues.

In the realm of politics, women became increasingly visible by the mid-1990s. The 1995 and 2000 parliamentary elections not only resulted in more women members of Parliament but also in the emergence of articulate reform-minded advocates.

5.10 Features and Discourses of Women's Movements

However, an analysis of discourses of women's movement which brought relative success in achieving women's demands and rights compared to Khomeini period as indicted above reflect the following features:

First, 'while the strategy of women's groups in pre-revolutionary periods was based on participation in a general social movement against the state, as expressed in anti-government demonstrations in the late 1970s and early 1980s, the strategy adopted by women activists in the post-Khomeini period involves accommodation, negotiation, and resistance'. [53] These strategies were gradual and focused. Women activists focused on specific issue and aimed for smaller but sustainable changes. They are concerned with tangible issues affecting their lives, such as the right of divorce, child custody, and inheritance. During this period women organisations and groups avoided the temptations of nation-cantered grand ideologies, theories and narratives to make significant changes in their lives and preferred a constitutional strategy from within the system with a view to appeal the conscience of *ulema* to bring necessary reform in gender policy that would help them to preserve their identities and dignity. Currently, a major effort is underway by women activists, both inside and outside of the state, to have the Islamic Republic join the

United Nations' Convention on the Elimination of All Forms of Discrimination against Women (CEDAW).

Second, there is greater individualism in the current women's activism than has existed anytime before in the past century—an attitude grounded in and fostered by the globalizing forces of modernity. [54] The state's efforts for imposing a collectivist identity on Iranian women backfired and gave rise to a desire to find a balance between the extremes of Western individualism and Islamic collectivism. Gradually, more and more women tried to de-link their identity from group affiliations (i.e., religion, family, and ethnicity) and emphasized their individuality based on their own achievements.

Third, issues and interests energizing the new Iranian women's movement are nuanced and varied. They include a greater awareness of human rights, individual rights, individual autonomy within marriage, family independence within the kinship network, and a form of national consciousness against the global diffusion of modern values. The movement can be best characterized as 'collective action without actors'. [55] The past dependency of women's activism on male organization has been replaced by a highly confident attitude and determination to fight this battle for women's rights mostly by women themselves. There were significant upsurge among women in forming their own organizations, forums, groups away and separate from men's organizations. These collective efforts and groupings helped them to debate universal and national issues from their own particularistic perspective so that their specific concerns receive focused attention.

Fourth, in the latter part of the 1990s, an alliance of secular and Islamic feminists began to contest the institutionalized privileges of men over women. Although common ground exists among women's rights activists, political and ideological differences remain. Lines of demarcation divide secular from Islamist feminists. Secular feminists are opposed to the Islamic

Constitution and to *Shari'a* based family and law codes. Instead, they seek complete separation of religion from state and legal frameworks. In contrast, Islamist feminists seek reform of religious-based laws by contesting traditional and patriarchal interpretations of the *Qur'an* in favour of alternative interpretations, and they emphasize its emancipatory and egalitarian content. Most secular feminists use the language of liberal democracy to emphasize political freedoms for the country and personal freedoms for women. Last but not the least, the women movement in Iran by late 1990s moved from mobilizing section of *Ulema* to influence the government decision in their favour to the political strategy of directly sending the female candidates in the Parliament.

5.11 Return of Repression and Exclusion under Ahmadinejad

It was this new found confidence during Rafsanjani and Khatami period that women movements in Iran sustained the brutal crackdown of Ahmadinejad government upon them. The 2005 election of Ahmadinejad and his policies dampened women's activism. In 2005, about a hundred women managed to enter Tehran's soccer stadium to watch a game between the national teams of Iran and Bahrain. [56] The women's rights activist declared June 12 to be Women's Solidarity Day and held an unauthorized demonstration in Tehran. It was the first such demonstration since 1979 revolution, as they chanted, "we are women, we are children of this land, but we have no rights". [57]

The June 2005 protest was a turning point [58] for female activism where new activist strategies and patterns were established. Firstly, despite the lack of government approval for the sit-in participation was high. Notwithstanding the encirclement by police officers, the incidence of violence was limited as the police opted for the strategy of containment of the demonstration. Secondly, the activist message was not limited to a certain class or age group of women but rather extended to all Iranian women. Thirdly, NGO's and independent associations, students, journalists, bloggers all came together and brought attention to the declaration demanding that the nation's laws secure women's fundamental and equal rights and comply with international conventions such as CEDAW.

Upon his election twelve days later, President Ahmadinejad changed the name of the Centre for Women's Participation to the Centre for Women and Family Affairs, and directed that female government employees only work during daylight hours—once again emphasizing the role of women as housewives and mothers, details of which are given in fourth chapter of the thesis. Women demonstrated on International Women's Day (March 8) in 2006, and were beaten and arrested by baton-wielding police. They attempted to gather again on June 12 of that year, but were arrested and dispersed before they could assemble. The Judiciary announced the arrest of seventy people including Fariba Davoudi Mohajer, Shahla Entesari, Parvin Ardalan, Noushin Ahmadi Khorasani and Sussan Tahmasebi, and charged them with crimes ranging from acting against state security to propaganda against the state. [59]

Following that year's June 12 demonstration, activists created the Campaign for Equality that launched the Campaign for the Collection of One Million Signatures to Reform Discriminatory Laws against Women. Officially launched on August 27, 2006, the Campaign aims to obtain the signatures of one million Iranians in support of amendments to the country's civil and penal codes. [60] The regime regularly shut down the One Million Signatures Campaign's websites, beat and arrested demonstrators, and interrogated and harassed its activists. Increasingly, phones and e-mails were monitored. [61] However, the Campaign's grassroots nature allowed it to withstand state pressure and continue to build broad-based support.

In April 2007, then-intelligence minister Qolam-Hossein Mohseni Ejei claimed [62] that the women's rights movement was part of an attempt by outside enemies to bring about the soft overthrow of the Islamic Republic. The regime shut down organizations as well as print media and websites. In November, the regime banned publication of *Zanestan,* a website run by the Women's Cultural Centre. In January 2008, the authorities shut down *Zanan,* which had been one of the most important women's magazines in Iran. Officials claimed it "endangered the spiritual, mental and intellectual health of its readers, gave the impression of insecurity in society, and drew a dark image of the situation of women in Islamic society by publishing certain articles". [63]

In 2009, the Guardian Council again rejected the candidacies of women in the presidential election. [64] However, opposition candidate platforms and positions often included issues of female equality that reflected pressure from women's rights groups. The regime responded by arresting, interrogating, imprisoning, and harassing activists and their defenders. The "Coalition of the Women's Movement to Set Forth Demands in the Election" made two fundamental demands of the presidential candidates: (i) that Iran ratify the Convention on the Elimination of all Forms of Discrimination Against Women (CEDAW), and (ii) that they try to "remove all discriminatory laws against women and especially revision and amendment of Articles 19, 20, 21 and 115 of the Constitution in order to include the principle of unconditional gender equality. [65]

Women's rights activists attended election rallies and distributed literature setting forth these demands. Three of the four candidates, recognizing the electoral potential of such a significant segment of the population, increasingly spoke out on issues that mattered to women of all backgrounds. Reformist candidate Mir-Hossein Mousavi issued a 'comprehensive and detailed' plan to promote gender equality through measures that included ratification of the CEDAW and ensuring greater access for women to higher education and professional fields. Reformist candidate Mehdi Karroubi issued a statement in May 2009 in which he pledged, *inter alia*, to review discriminatory laws, ensure women held decision-making positions in government, and implement CEDAW. Conservative candidate Mohsen Rezai promised that he would appoint female ministers, provide salaries to housewives, promote women's organizations, and facilitate the fair distribution of opportunities to men and women. [66]

Zahra Rahnavard, in her position as the wife of reformist candidate Mousavi, broke precedent by campaigning publicly with her husband—the first candidate's wife in the history of the Islamic Republic to do so. Rahnavard used the spotlight of her husband's campaign to convey a platform of expanded women's rights, including "elimination of discrimination and strengthening of cultural rights, women's rights and equal rights under the law". [67] Rahnavard also publicly endorsed the One Million Signatures Campaign and published an article calling for an end to discrimination against women and pushing for ratification of international women's rights conventions.

5.12 Resilience and Strength of Women's Movements

However, the incumbent regime increased its suppression of women's rights activists and organizations during the lead-up to the 2009 elections. It shut down offices, arrested and interrogated many activists, and prevented some from leaving the country. Ahmadinejad's crackdown raises a pertinent question vis-à-vis women's movement in Iran: Is there a cohesive social movement of women that can bring about the necessary legal and political reforms to accompany the very real social changes that have occurred in Iran? There are two schools of thought on this issue. Ali Akbar Mahdi and others have argued that women have created a movement "without direction, leadership, and structure". At the same time, according to Mahdi, this movement reveals women's "greater awareness of human rights, individual rights, individual autonomy within marriage, family independence within the kinship network, and a form of national consciousness against the global diffusion of Western values". [68]

On the other hand Farhad Khosrowkhavar describes the

women's movement in Iran as one of the three new social movements to emerge in the late 1990s; the other two being students and intellectuals. [69] These are portrayed as post-ideological, post-class movements, although an alternative perspective might regard them as liberal, middle-class movements. Different from these two schools Valentine M. Moghadam [70] considers women movement in Iran in a pre-movement phase, without the large public mobilizations and independent organizations needed to constitute a social movement.

Women in the Islamic Republic are not passive. They are active and engage in the politics of resistance. They exert pressure on the system, pose important questions, express their concerns, and above all demand that they have rights as women and citizens. Not only do they seek responses to their interests, but they search for alternative ways to amend if not modify policies, thereby moving the wheels of incremental transformation. Active women are diverse and their activities intersect with their class background, ideology, the degree of their religious identity, and the geographical setting of their environment. More secular and middle-class, many urban opponent women redefine veiling practices and gender policies almost daily. They utilize innovative tactics and engage in unprecedented creative methods to challenge policies, and more slowly the parameters of the system itself. Whether pro-regime or anti-establishment, urban or rural, well off or less privileged, religious or secular, active women are diverse and their experiences complex. The convergence of secular and religious women on many issues related to women has posed an unexpected challenge before the Islamic regime. Though the gender bias remains strong in the Islamic republic of Iran, however women's activism and awareness has resulted in the gradual loosing of state's control over women through the instrument of resistance and negotiations.

Endnotes

1. For details see, chapter 2, "Imam Khomeini and Construction of

Islamic Republic of Iran: Implications for Iranian Women", pp. 11-22.
2. Yeganeh, Nahid (1982), "Women's Struggle in Islamic Republic of Iran", in 'The Shadow of Islam: The Women's Movement in Iran', Azar Tabari and Nahid Yeganeh (eds.), p. 35, London: Zed Books.
3. Paider, Parvin (1995), "Women and the Political Process in Twentieth Century Iran", p. 234, Cambridge: Cambridge University Press.
4. Ibid.
5. Mahdi, Ali Akbar (2004), "The Iranian Women's Movement: A Century Long Struggle", *Journal of the Muslim World,* Vol. 94, October, p. 434.
6. Hoodfar, Homa (1999), "The Women's Movement in Iran: Women at the Crossroads of Secularization and Islamisation", in The Women's Movement Series No.1, Women Living under Muslim Laws: International Solidarity Network, International Solidarity Network, Grabels Cedex, France, p. 24, available at: wrrc.wluml.org/sites/wluml.org/files/.../women-movement-iran-eng.pdf.
7. Hoodfar, Homa and Sadr, Shadi (2009), "Can Women Act as Agents of a Democratization of Theocracy in Iran"?, final research report prepared for the project Religion, Politics and Gender Equality, United Nations Research Institute for Social Development (UNRISD) and Heinrich-Böll-Stiftung, p. 15, available at: http://www.unrisd.org/80256B3C005BCCF9/search/2E975ACA2A81AA54C12576580028735C?OpenDocument.
8. Ibid.
9. Ibid.
10. Bayat, Asef (2007), "A Women's Non-Movement: What It Means to Be a Woman Activist in an Islamic State", *Comparative Studies of South Asia, Africa and the Middle East,* No. 1, p. 162.
11. Ibid.
12. Ibid.
13. Ibid., p. 163.
14. Paider, No. 3, p. 240.
15. Halper, Louise (2005), "Law and Women's Agency in Post-revolutionary Iran", *Harvard Journal of Law and Gender,* Vol.

28, p. 111.
16. Ibid.
17. Hoodfar and Sadr, No. 7, p. 22.
18. Ibid.
19. Ibid., p. 20.
20. Ibid.
21. Ibid.
22. Ibid., p. 22.
23. Hoodfar, No. 6, p. 28.
24. Hoodfar, Homa and Sadeghi, Fatemeh (2009), "Against All Odds: The Building of a Women's Movement in the Islamic Republic of Iran", p. 4, available at: http://r4d.dfid.gov.uk/PDF/Outputs/WomenEmpMus/Hoodfar_AgainstAllOdds_Iran.pdf.
25. See, Bayat, Asef (2007), "Making Islam Democratic: Social Movements and the Post-Islamist Turn", Stanford: Stanford University Press.
26. Louise, No. 15, p. 112.
27. Hoodfar, No. 6, p. 30.
28. Ibid.
29. Paider, No. 3, p. 311.
30. Hoodfar and Sadr, No. 7, p. 29.
31. Paider, No. 3, p. 311.
32. Ibid., p. 30.
33. Ibid.
34. Ibid., p. 32.
35. *Iran Times*,13.6.86, quoted in Paider, No. 3, p. 284.
36. For the data, see Hoodfar, No. 6, p. 36.
37. Mahdi, No. 5, p. 437.
38. Amin, Camron Michael (2002), "The Making of the Modern Iranian Woman: Gender, State Policy, and Popular Culture, 1865-1946", Gainesville, FL: University Press of Florida.
39. For an analysis of women in Marxist organizations in the 1970s, see Moghissi, Haideh (1994), "Populism and Feminism in Iran: Women's Struggle in a Male-Defined Revolutionary Movement", New York: St. Martin's Press.
40. Tabari, Azar (1982), "Islam and the Struggle for Emancipation of Women", in Azar Tabari and Nahid Yeganeh (eds.), 'In the Shadow of Islam; The Women's Movement in Iran', p. 16, London: Zed Press.

41. See Hoodfar and Sadr, No. 7, p. 15.
42. Ibid., p. 25.
43. Ibid.
44. Ibid.
45. Ibid.
46. Mir-Hosseini, Ziba (2002), "Religious Modernists and the Woman Question: Challenges and Complicities", in 'Twenty Years of Islamic Revolution: Political and Social Transition in Iran since 1979', Eric Hooglund (ed.), p. 75, Syracuse University Press.
47. Razavi, Shahra (2006), "Islamic Politics, Human Rights and Women's Claims for Equality in Iran", *Third World Quaterly,* Vol. 27, No. 7, p. 1227.
48. Ibid.
49. Ibid.
50. Najmabadi, Afsaneh (Un)Veiling Feminism, available at: http://muse.jhu.edu/journals/soc/summary/v018/18.3najmabadi.html.
51. For the above data, see Moghadam, Valentine M., "Women in the Islamic Republic of Iran: Legal Status, Social Positions and Collective Action", available at: http://www.wilsoncenter.org/sites/default/files/ValentineMoghadamFinal.pdf.
52. For the data on women's education, see Rezai, Goli M., "The Future of Iran: Educational Reform Women and Education in the Islamic Republic of Iran: Repressive Policies, Unexpected Outcomes", available at: http://www.li.com/docs/default-source/default-document-library/women-and-education-in-the-islamic-republic-of-iran-repressive-policies-unexpected-outcomes.
53. Mahdi, No .5, p. 442.
54. Ibid., p. 443.
55. Ibid.
56. Vakil, Sanam (2012), "Women and Politics in the Islamic Republic of Iran: Action and Reaction", p. 159, Bloomsbury Academic.
57. Fathi, Nazila, "Hundreds of Women Protest Sex Discrimination in Iran", New York Times, June 12, 2005, available at: http://www.nytimes.com/2005/06/12/international/middleeast/13womencnd.html.

58. Vakil, No. 56, p. 159.
59. For the above paragraph, see Iran Human Rights Documentation Centre (IHRDC), "Silencing the Women's Rights Movement in Iran", available at: http://www.iranhrdc.org/english/publications/reports/3007-silencing-the-women-s-rights-movement-in-iran.html?p=8.
60. Ibid.
61. Ibid.
62. Ibid., p. 9.
63. Ibid., p. 10.
64. Ibid., p. 12.
65. Ibid., pp. 8-10.
66. Ibid., p. 13.
67. Ibid.
68. Mahdi, Ali Akbar, "Iranian Women: Between Islamicization and Globalization", available at: go.owu.edu/~aamahdi/womenpercent20andpercent20globalization-final.pdf.
69. Moghadam, No. 51, p. 9.
70. Ibid.

6

Conclusions

There is an intricate relationship between religion, gender, sexuality and nation. Traditionally, the relationship between these categories or variables has mostly been analyzed from the instrumental perspective in which the state uses them politically to construct an 'imagined' nation. However this work, while highlighting the political use of religion, gender and sexuality by the Islamic state of Iran to construct a particular Iranian Islamic nation state, goes beyond this traditional understanding of relationship between religion, gender, sexuality and state. It demonstrates that relationship among them does not merely envisage a 'top-down structure' or 'bottom-top structures' but rather is one of dyadic and interactive process. The interactive process between the two also partly flows from an understanding that the state is not a single-minded actor with a unified set of interests. On the contrary any state consists of different, sets of factions and interests without having any fixed relationship with gender although dominant (male) gender grossly influence the discourse of state. Thus, the interplay of gender-identity, religion, class, ideologies and political participation of women in the context of Iran has clearly brought out its implication for negotiating the privileges and rights of women with the existing polity and power structure and shifting nature of nation-building process in post Khomeini Iran.

The linkage between gender and nation is mediated through the administrative agency of state. As the identity of nation is far from settled in most of societies, particularly in post-colonial societies, it is the state that fashion and refashions the construction of nation building process in the society. It is in this process of politics of 'imagined' community', to use the phrase of Benedict Anderson, [1] that various governments differentially impacts on the gender relationship in the society depending upon its ideological world-view, social base and nature of factional politics. Thus, state or government uses women and their portrayal to ensure the multiple purposes: depict a distinct political identity of the 'imagined' nation- such as secular or religious, traditional or modern or westernized and Islamized, to legitimize its cultural and political position/values and to consolidate its power. In the process state sets an agenda for the control of particular class of women or their activities and unleashes the programme for expanding or contracting gender specific opportunity structure. Thus, the state plays an important role in modifying and restructuring gender relations and accordingly builds alliances with different classes of women especially in their politics of mobilization.

The Islamic Republic of Iran since its foundation reveals the similar pattern of relationship between the various governments and gender to achieve the above listed objectives. By employing the perspective of 'gender studies' and 'gendering politics' the present work also highlights the limitations of two contesting school of thoughts (broadly speaking) that have sought to examine the question of women rights in contemporary Iran within the conventional perspective of women studies. The first school argues that religion, particularly Islam, is inherently anti-women and tends to highlight the marginalized and subordinate position of women in Iranian society under Islamic Republic in comparison to Shah's period. The other school of thought argues that religion including Islam does not obstruct the development of women and women in Islamic Republic of Iran has achieved far greater rights and privileges whether in field of education, political participation, employment vis-à-vis Shah regime. However, unlike these two schools of thought, this work demonstrates that how through the process 'gendering politics' women act as 'lively citizenry' and negotiate with the existing power structure of Islamic Republic of Iran in the post-Khomeini period that sometimes results in contraction of their rights and privileges and sometimes expands the same depending upon the nature of political regime and socio-economic-political context.

The principle of contraction and expansion of women rights within the Islamic Republic of Iran moves both horizontally and vertically depending upon the socio-economic and political context as well as the factor of 'imagined nation'. In horizontal terms, the variation in the contraction and expansion of women rights was evident, from one regime to another within the Islamic republic of Iran. Thus Iran witnessed a shift from relatively closed vision of Islam that imposed restrictions on the life styles of women in Iran to relatively open/liberal vision of Islam under Rafsanjani and Khatami's period that helped in easing out many of the restrictions placed upon the women during Khomeini's period as well as increasing the visibility of women in the public life before relapsing again into strict regulation of women's life during Ahmadinejad period. For instance, whereas during Khomeini and Ahmadinejad period the practice of family planning was denounced and declared un-Islamic, under the Rafsanjani and Khatami period Iran witnessed the most successful implementation of family planning that was duly acknowledged by UN body.

In vertical terms, the variation in contraction and expansion of women rights took place within the span of a single regime. Thus the decade old, national context of Iran-Iraq War and protection of Islamic Republic against imperialism was used by Khomeini in curtailing or in implementing retrogressive laws towards women, which was in part also linked with his imagination of Islamic Iranian nation. Khomeini was forced to concede to women as he confronted the realities of state and war. To retain female support he enfranchised women. Compulsory veiling, the ban on women singers, exclusion from political power, economic marginalization and the return of unilateral divorce, promotion of polygamy and temporary marriage were some of the major gender policies as detailed in the preceding chapter that characterized the first ten years of the Islamic Revolution. However, towards the end of life in the context of emerging oppositional voices, women's movement and the necessities of the economy forced Khomeini to concede many of the demands by either withdrawing or amending the retrogressive policies that enunciated from time to time during his regime. Further, Islamic vision of Khomeini did not hamper the access of girls to education; rather the regime facilitated and resulted in the unprecedented educational development of women compared to Pahlavi Shah's period and contrary to western public perception. Women at the same time used Khomeini's early dispensations towards women in an effort to reverse patriarchal legal interpretations and secure political, economic and legal concessions.

The nature of gender politics within the Islamic frame underwent significant changes under the regimes of Rafsanjani and Khatami. Whereas during the Khomeini period gender related issue was looked upon primarily from ideological point of view, during Rafsanjani and Khatami period the issue of gender was framed/looked in a less ideological way and more guided by pragmatic considerations. It was the interplay of socio economic and political context at national and international level along with the relative Islamic liberal ideas of Rafsanjani and Khatami that structured the nature of gender politics in Iran during this period. Thus lack of charismatic leadership following the death of Ayatollah Khomeini in 1989, constitutional amendment leading to strong president and weak *Velayat-e-Faqih*, the disastrous impact of international economic sanctions and decade old Iran-Iraq War on the national economy, the consideration to end the international isolation of Iran led to development of more plural voices within Islamic Republic of Iran.

As a result, during this period, women's movement gained new voices and increased their visibility in public spheres and was largely successful in mobilizing the political leadership to conceive their demands. Women's participation in the various walks of life—social, political and economic—vastly improved. There was tremendous improvement in the development of women on all human indicators, the details of which have already been noted in the third and fifth chapter of the thesis. Thus, during

Rafsanjani's period many barriers to women's educational achievement and their employment were removed. Women were encouraged to enter certain scientific and technical fields such as gynaecology, pharmacology, midwifery and the laboratory work etc. In 1992, a law allowed women to sit as assistant judges in courts hearing divorce cases. The 1992 Family Law made it mandatory that marriage contract can list stipulations under which women can initiate divorce. A notable achievement of the Rafsanjani regime was successful family planning programme that was even acknowledged by UN agency.

The Khatami regime continued this trend and even saw the more robust growth and vitality of Iranian civil society and a movement for political and cultural reform. In 1997, for the first time, a woman was appointed as a judge after the establishment of Islamic Republic. Women's *mehrieh* became exempted from the taxes. In the academic year 2002-2003 women's university enrolments exceeded those of men for the first time since universities were established in Iran. In 2002, single women received permission to study abroad on government fellowships and the return of women to the courts as consultative judges. Numerous women's organizations, bureaus, offices and commissions were also formed. Winning publication, reformist, gender journals and magazines blossomed. Khatami regime was noted for a remarkable cultural freedom that Iranian women enjoyed. Through these mediums women addressed their demands as well as discussed cultural gender inequities. Such dialogues were also enhanced by the growth of the internet.

However, despite a reformist decade the legal framework remained very unfavourable for women. Women still faced numerous discriminatory policies and practices. For example, forced veiling subjects women to harsh penalties for non-compliance. Women still needed father's legal permission to get married. Father still has the exclusive right of child custody in case of divorce. Inheritance law still favours men. The custom of *mut'a* (temporary) marriage continued to flourish and even received encouragement from the Rafsanjani government. Similarly the Khatami regime could not succeed in getting CEDAW and right to inheritance bill passed in the Iranian parliament. Also number of elected female member in the parliament declined during the Khatami era.

On the other hand the interplay of social, economic, political and ideological factors influenced or shaped the Ahmadinejad government to roll back many of the gains that women had achieved during the previous two regimes. This included his own exclusive Islamic ideas, the increasing hostility of US and Israel to the Iranian nuclear programme and the rise of conservative IRGC (Iranian Republican Guards Corps), which is conservative force on women issues and considers itself as the heir of Imam Khomeini's legacy. In addition to illegal arrest, torture and harassment of women rights activists, the Ahmadinejad government extolled a greater resort to polygamy as a solution to pervasive female unemployment, closed down the veteran women's magazine *Zanan* in 2008 and the same year the Parliament finally granted the right to inherit land from their deceased husbands. Notwithstanding the setback to women's movement and women rights and violation of human rights, there have been significant improvements in the women's education, health along with a remarkable drop in the birth rates. Women became the Minister for the first time in the history of Islamic Republic of Iran. Thus, even Ahmadinejad could not isolate women and ignore gender issues.

This horizontal and vertical expansion and contraction of women rights in Iran partly also emanates from the contradictory pulls and pressures resulting from constitutional recognition of women as 'political citizen' that gives her entitlement to participate in the political-public sphere on the one hand and thrust of 'imagined Islamic nation state' that confines the Iranian women to private family sphere while offering the limited role in political-public sphere. This contradictory pulls and pressure has been witnessed in all Islamic regimes of Iran, though they differ in terms of degree depending upon the context and specific imagination of Islamic nation-state.

This principal finding of the present work also contradicts the pervasive modernist view that religion, particularly Islam, obstructs the development of women in the various field of life. In particular it asserts that Islam is not a monolithic phenomenon and demonstrates that women movements are not singular, but plural in orientations. Even in the religious imagination, as is commonly understood, women is not considered a mere a passive creature and an object of sexual reproduction but a very active agency to be fully participant in the social, economic and political life of the country. Thus, the Islamic Republic did not inherit a readymade Islamic policy on gender. The dominant conceptions of gender were constructed as events developed in post-revolutionary society and demonstrate the variations in women responses to the specific gender policy of the particular regime.

This study also highlights the plural face of *ulema* and underlines the conflictual relationship between conservative *ulema* who favour the domestication of women and the progressive *ulema* which fights to safeguard and expand women's rights. Thus, Islam is not monolithic as there is deeper internal contestation about the normative values of Islam, which in turn has implications for inter-gender relations as well as gender-state relation as reflected in the preceding chapters of this thesis. The non-monolithic character of Islam also partly explains that there is no uniformity in terms of impact of public policy on power relationship between gender in the Iranian context. It varies from one regime to another despite the fact that there is a consensus that women is an important marker of national identity which enjoins that the Iranian polity must regulate her life and also prescribes the mode of interaction between the sexes.

The key to understanding the gender discourse in Islamic Republic of Iran is interpretative field of Islam that legitimizes and delegitimizes various actions of state including its gender related programme and policies. From Imam Khomeini to Ahmadinejad—all testifies that there is no 'monolithic, fixed Islamic gender ideology' that determines and legitimizes the gender policies of Islamic Republic of Iran. All post-Khomeini regimes used Islamic narratives to legitimize the state policies intended to either liberalize or de-liberalize the Islamic values that impinges on the lives of Iranian women. Thus even though all regimes—right from Khomeini to Ahmadinejad—are Islamic; their Islamic understanding of the nation varies that itself has an implication in terms of hardening or relaxing the Islamic codes while claiming the authenticity of Islamic identity of nation-state.

The Islamic state's mission has been to create an ideal Islamic society wherein women and men can accomplish their holy duties. As the family is regarded as the microcosm of ideal Islamic society, the Islamic government in Iran has considered it pivotal to "strengthen the family" in order to realize its imagined Islamic nation. The prominent place that was given to the women and family in the Constitution of Islamic Republic of Iran testifies the commitments to realize the goal of constructing an ideal Islamic nation. The Constitution considered women and family as the main element in the identity of the Islamic nation.

It clearly demonstrates that the Islamic nation was dependent on the Islamization of gender relations. It constructed a new "Islamic" link between nation and gender and specified a corresponding position for women. Women were constructed as citizens in the interest of the nation building, but they were also defined in their special roles within the state and community. Women were defined as biological reproducers of the community and nation and were assigned roles on this basis. Women remained at the centre of Islamic discourses in the IRI since the inception of foundation of IRI as preservation of national identity, the thrust of which varies from regime to regime, becomes equivalent to protecting and controlling women's sexuality. Thus, the control of women's sexuality has become a core of the power struggle between the ideologically rival groups in the Iranian political system. As Fatima Mernissi has noted that the sexual power attributed to women has caused the Islamic states to contain and control their sexuality through such social institutions such as the veil, the family, the marriage system and the legal system. [2]

All gender-specific policies of Islamic Republic of Iran from Imam Khomeini to Ahmadinejad have operated within this constitutional limit of role of women and family in the construction of 'Islamic nationhood' in Iran. Notwithstanding the differences in the Islamic vision of conservatives and reformists vis-à-vis the role and status of women in Iranian society, religious imperatives constitute a fundamental concern for all Islamists—conservatives and reformist alike. Both believe in women's familial role, natural basis of sex roles, and the assumption that women needs protection. To accomplish these aims the conservatives propose seclusion, reformers a "safe", regulated social-political space for women. An analysis of fifty random interview that was conducted from Iranian women in order to elicit the women's perception about the existing Islamic state in Iran did confirm the variation in the application of Islamic rules and regulations vis-à-vis gender from one regime to another. The majority of female interviewee prefers Khatami and Rafsanjani regime in comparison to Ahmadinejad regime and expects more just and equal treatment in the name of Islam. In addition, the majority of women do not challenge the Islamic legitimacy of state.

The gender policies of the state ranging from Imam Khomeini to Ahmadinejad era and their impact on women as detailed in the preceding chapters broadly covers three major categories. The first set is the policies which were/are aimed fundamentally at women. This includes the protective legislation and reproduction such as abortion laws, family planning, temporary marriage and maternity leave.

A second set of policies relates to the relation between men and women, particularly property rights, family relations, matrimonial rights, labour laws, areas where power relations between men and women are and therefore gender relations are often institutionalized. The laws and regulations surrounding these issues become an area of contestation when attempts are made to alter the existing pattern of power relationships as occurred and women's mobility become highly contested. The third set of policies—general and gender neutral—have and different impact on women and men. This involves the developmental programme of the government such as setting up industry, communication, transportation, defence, health facility, law and order machinery, education etc that are conceived in gender-neutral framework but have differential impact on gender.

Although the state possess the capacity to modify and reshape gender relations and women's lives, its actions, however, are also limited by the persistence of women's resistance. As active social agency women respond, defy and pose challenges to the state's action, which either results in the favourable or negative public policy outcome depending upon the political context. The responses of women vary historically depending upon their class background, ideological dispositions, rural-urban location, educational attainment, religious outlook and degree of their political and feminist awareness. The women' movement in Islamic Republic of Iran demonstrates the similar trajectory where it has moved through the phases of collaboration, conciliation, and confrontation using diverse tactics to advance their agenda for women's equality. Women activism has flourished in response and in reaction to the contradictory policies of the government, which created space for women to negotiate. This trend has been detailed under fifth chapter of the thesis.

Many women supporters of the Khomeini regime soon realized that the idealized notion of an Islamic way of life had helped to create a political order that legally undermined women in marriage, family and the work place. Many Islamist women (commonly known as Islamic feminists) also became the advocates of women's rights and register their protest to the

Khomeini regime. The post-Khomeini period witnessed the more robust kind of women movements and opposition resulting in many innovative and entrepreneurial characteristics of women's activism.

This included the publication of many feminist magazines (*Zanan, Farzaneh, Jens-e Dovvom* etc) criticizing the subordinate status of women in the Islamic Republic and calling for the modernizing the family law; academicians forming women's studies courses or programs at the universities, the growth of NGO'S devoted to women's empowerment, and the emergence of Islamic feminism whereby women sought to frame their demands for their rights in religious idioms and to recover their religion from patriarchal interpretations.

In the run up to the elections of 2005, the women movements were mobilized to take the call for women's equality in the family and the society to the streets, demanding equality in family issues, an end to stoning as a punishment for real sexual transgression, and the ratification of the UN's Convention of all Forms of Discrimination against women (CEDAW) along with the abrogation of all gender discriminatory laws in Iran. The call for gender equality continued despite the brutal crackdown by the Ahmadinejad government on the women's movement. The state repression forced the women's movement to devise a new strategy in 2006 for legal and policy change: the One Million Signature petition campaign. This was a door-to-door campaign to obtain signatures for the abrogation of all discriminatory laws and provide women with equality in home and in society.

One consequence of the women' movement in Iran since Khomeini's period is that the ideological division between the secular feminist movement, the Islamic feminist movement and pro government Islamic women movement that has marred the unity of women's movement vis-à-vis Islamic regime began to crumble by the end of Ahmadinejad government as they came to realize that their concern and demands are the more or less same and irrespective of ideological position they all suffer as 'women' from the anti-women policies of the

Islamic regimes. This unity of approach was reflected in their overwhelming support to Mr. Rouhani during the Presidential election of 2014.

The 'gendering politics' in Iran helps in democratizing the social and political process with a view to ensure the more meaningful participation of women in formal as well as informal spaces. The impact of gendering politics in Iran in terms of democratizing the social and political process is evident from the failure of Ahmadinejad government to completely roll back the privileges and rights of women in Iran, which they had gained through the strategy of negotiations with the Islamic polity since Ayatollah Khomeini times. Though the overall goal of 'gendering politics' is to usher into a gender friendly or gender-neutral nation building process, it would be difficult to argue in the light of analysis of this thesis that any substantial progress has been made in this direction in Islamic Republic of Iran, though women's movements in Iran-whether secular or Islamic—aspires for the same as evident from many statements of important individuals connected with women's movement and organisations. However, the gendering politics from Khomeini to Ahmadinejad regime has resulted in overall terms in diluting or reducing the power gap between the genders as evident from the enhanced position of women in various field of life.

Endnotes

1. Anderson, Benedict (2007), "Imagined Communities: Reflections on the Origin and Spread of Nationalism", Verso Books.
2. Quoted in Sedghi, Hamideh (2007), "Women and Politics in Iran: Veiling, Unveiling, and Reveiling", p. 13, Cambridge University Press.

Glossary

Ayatollah	Sign of God.
Bad-hejabi	Improper veiling.
Bazaari	Mercantile/trader.
Chador	It literally means a tent. It's a long veil that covers women from head to toe and is normally held under the chin.
Diyeh	Blood money.
Fatwa	Religious edict. Opinion exerted by a *mojtahed* or *faqih* on any matter.
Faqih	A high ranking cleric who is an expert on *fiqh (feqh)*.
Feqh	Islamic Jurisprudence.
feqh-e pooya	Dynamic Islamic Jurisprudence.
feqh-e sonnati	Tradition belonging to Prophet Muhammad and his companions based jurisprudence.
Ghanun	Retribution for killing or injuring another
Ghesas	party.
Hadith	The collected record of sayings and actions of the Prophet. The *Hadith* ranks second in importance to the *Qur'an* as the basis of the Islamic *feqh*.
Hejab	It literally means curtain or screen. It refers to the women's Islamic covering. It is described as a type of women's clothing which protects her body from the eyes of men who are forbidden to her. The exact form of *hejab* varies, but is regarded in its current usage to include a headscarf, a loose and long dress which is high at the neck and has long sleeves, and a pair of trousers under it to cover the legs. Women who do not fully observe the *hejab* are called *bad hejab*.

Hejab-e eslam	*A form of* Islamic dress.
Hojatoleslam	The sign of God. A title given to recognized ulama.
Howzeh	Seminary.
Iddeh	A period of celibacy immediately after divorce or the death of a husband during which a woman may not remarry. This is normally for three menstrual cycles, and its purpose is to determine whether the woman is bearing a child from her previous marriage.
Ijtihad	An Islamic principle of right to reinterpret the Islamic texts (principally Qur'an and Hadith) to be exercised by the designated *Mojtahed.*
Jihad	Literally means struggle. Religious duty of all Muslims to pursue as spiritual struggle to understand the faith.
Jens-Dovom	Second sex.
Khanevadeh	Family.
Komitehs	Grouping of local enforces and moral police established after the 1979 Revolution.
Majles	The Iranian Parliament.
Marja'e Taqlid	The highest source of imitation within the *Shi'i* faith.
Maqna'eh	A tight scarf that covers all hair, neck and shoulders.
Mehrieh (Mahr)	The bride price agreed between the families of the bride and groom and included in the marriage contract.
Mojtahed	A *Shi'i* cleric who has attained the highest level of religious knowledge and expertise enabling him to practice ijtihad. Each mojtahed has his own followers and can use his own *fatwas*.

Nafagheh	Alimony payable by a husband to a wife if she has child custody.
Ojrat-ol mesal	Wages for house work.
Qur'an (Koran)	The Islamic holy book which Muslims consider the words of God.
Roopoosh	Loose tunic worn over clothing.
Shari'a	Islamic law encompasses the totality of Islamic jurisprudence.
Shi'ism	A branch of Islam whose founders were the partisans and follower of the Prophet's son-in law, Ali. *Shi'i* believes that after the Prophet's death the leadership of Islam should have been transferred to Ali. There are many branches of *Shi'ism,* the dominant form of which is Twelver Ithna Ashari. Twelver *Shi'ism* has been the official religion of Iran since the sixteenth century.
Sigheh (mut'a)	Temporary marriage.
Sunnah	Tradition.
Taqlid	A source of religious emulation.
Ulema/clerics	Religious scholars.
Ummah	Community of believers/Muslims bound together by ties of religion.
Vali	Father or guardian.
Velayat-e Faqih	The guardianship of the Islamic jurisprudence. It refers to Ayatollah Khomeini's theory on the guardianship of the *faqih* as the head of the state in the absence of the twelfth Imam.
Zanan	Women.
Zan-e Ruz	Woman of today.
Zena	Adultery, fornication, sexual intercourse between men and women who are not married to each other. In Iran, *zena* is a crime punishable by flogging or stoning to death.

Bibliography

A. Primary Sources

Algar, Hamid (1980), "The Constitution of the Islamic Republic of Iran", (translation), Berkley: Mizan Press.

Centre for the Participation of Women (2003), "The Answer of the Government of the Islamic Republic of Iran to the Questionnaire to Governments on the Implementation of the Beijing Platform for Action(1995) and the Outcome of the Twenty-Third Special Session of the General Assembly (2000)", available at: http://www.un.org/womenwatch/daw/Review/responses/IRAN-English.pdf .

Mojtahedzadeh, Maryam (2013), Advisor to the President and Head of the Centre for Women and Family Affairs of Islamic Republic of Iran, speech at Commission on the Status of Women, New York, available at: http://www.un.org/womenwatch/daw/csw/csw57/generaldiscussion/memberstates/iran.pdf.

National AIDS Committee Secretariat, Ministry of Health and Medical Education (2012), "Islamic Republic of Iran AIDS Progress Report", available at: http://www.unaids.org/en/dataanalysis/knowyourresponse/countryprogressreports/2012countries/IRIr an%20AIDS%20Progress%20Report%202012%20English%20final1_1.pdf.

President's Deputy for Strategic Planning and Control and the United Nations (2006), "The Second Millennium Development Goals Report of the Islamic Republic of Iran", available at: http://www.undp.org.ir/doccenter/mdgs/Iran%20MDGs%20Report%2006-English.pdf.

United Nations Population Fund (UNFPA) (1998), "Country Report on Population, Reproductive Health and Family Planning Program in the Islamic Republic of Iran", Ministry of Health and Medical Education, Tehran.

UNHCR (2013a), "Country Operations Profile: Islamic Republic of Iran", available at: http://www.unhcr.org/pages/49e486f96.html.

World Bank (2013), "Gender Equality Data and Statistics", available

at:
http://datatopics.worldbank.org/gender.
World Bank (2013b), "Opening Doors: Gender Equality and Development in the Middle East and North Africa", MENA Development Report, Washington D.C., available at: https://openknowledge.worldbank.org/handle/10986/10844.
World Economic Forum (2012), "The Global Gender Gap Report", available at: http://www3.weforum.org/docs/WEF_GenderGap_Report_2012.pdf48.

B. Secondary Sources

B.1 Books

Abrahamian, Ervand (1982), "Iran between the Two Revolutions", Princeton University Press.
—1993, "Khomeinism: Essays on the Islamic Republic", Berkeley: University of California Press.
—1999, "Tortured Confessions: Prisons and Public Recantations in Modern Iran", Berkeley: University of California Press.
Abu-Lughod (ed) (1998), "Remaking Women: Feminism and Modernity in the Middle East", Princeton: Princeton University Press.
Afary, Janet (2009), "Sexual Politics in Iran", Cambridge University Press.
Afkhami, Mahnaz (1995), "Introduction in Faith and Freedom: Women's Human Rights in the Muslim World", New York: Syracuse University Press.
—and Friedl, Erika (1994), "In the Eyes of the: Women in Post-Revolutionary Iran", New York: Syracuse University Press.
Afshar, Haleh (1998), "Islam and Feminisms: An Iranian Case Study", New York: Palgrave.
—1996, "Women and Politics in Third World" (ed), Routledge.
Afshari, Reza (2011), "Human Rights in Iran: The Abuse of Cultural Relativism", University of Pennsylvania Press.
Agarwal, Bina (ed.) (1988), "Structures of Patriarchy: State, the Community and the Household", London: Zed Books.
Ahmed, Liela (1992), "Women and Gender in Islam: Historical Roots of Modern Debate", New Haven: Yale University Press.
—2012, "A Quiet Revolution: The Veil's Resurgence from the Middle East to America", Yale University Press.

Akhavi, Shahrough (1980), "Religion and Politics in Contemporary Iran: Clergy-State Relations in the Pahlavi Period", Albany: State University of New York Press.

Amin, Camron Michael (2002), "The Making of the Modern Iranian Woman: Gender, State Policy, and Popular Culture, 1865-1946", Gainesville, FL: University Press of Florida.

Anderson, Benedict (2007), "Imagined Communities: Reflections on the Origin and Spread of Nationalism", Verso Books.

Arjomand, Said Amir (1988), "The Turban for the Crown", Oxford: Oxford University Press.

Asgar, Fathi (ed) (1997), "Women and Family in Iran", Leiden: E.J. Brill.

Assad, Talal (1993), "Genealogies of Religion: Discipline and Reasons of Power in Christianity and Islam", Baltimore: The John Hopkins University Press.

Azari, Farah (ed) (1983), "Women of Iran: The Conflict with Fundamentalist Iran", London: Ithaca Press.

Badron, Margot (2008), "Feminism in Islam: Secular and Religious Convergences", Oxford: Oneworld Press.

Bahramitash, Roksana and Esfahani, Hadi Salehi (2011), "Veiled Employment: Islamism and Political Economy of Women's Employment in Iran", Syracuse University Press.

Bahrampour, Tara (1999), "To See and See Again: A Life in Iran and America", Farrar Straus and Giroux (T).

Bakhash, Shaul (1985), "The Reign of the Ayatollahs", New York: Basic Books.

Barnstein, Kate (1998), "My Gender Workbook", New York: Routledge.

Bayat, Asef (2010), "Life as Politics: How Ordinary People Change the Middle East/", Stanford: Stanford University Press.

—2007, "Making Islam Democratic: Social Movements and the Post-Islamist Turn", Stanford: Stanford University Press.

Benard, Cheryl and Khalilzad, Zalmay (1984), "The Government of God: Iran's Islamic Republic", New York: Columbia University Press.

Betteridge, Anne H. (1983), "To Veil or Not to Veil: A Matter of Protest or Policy", in 'Women and Revolution in Iran' (ed.), Guity Nashat, Boulder: Westview Press.

Birgit, Heller (2001), "Gender and Religion", in Børresen Kari Elisabeth (ed.), 'Gender and Religion', Roma: Carocci editore.

Boaz, Shoshan (2000), "Discourse on Gender/Gendered Discourse in the Middle East", London: Praeger.

Bonine, Michael and Keddie, Nikki (ed.) (1981), "Continuity and Change in Modern Iran", Albany: State University of New York Press.

Brooks, Geraldine (1995), "Nine Parts of Desire: The Hidden World of Islamic Women", Anchor Books.

Butler, Judith (1990), "Gender Trouble: Feminism and the Subversion of Identity", New York: Routledge.

Castelli, Elizabeth A. and Rodman, Rosamond C. (eds.) (2001), "Women, Gender, Religion: A Reader", New York: Palgrave.

Chatterjee, Partha (1993), "The Nation and its Fragments: Colonial and Post-Colonial Histories", Princeton University Press.

Chehabi, Houchang E. (1990), "Iranian Politics and Religious Modernism: The Liberation Movement of Iran under the Shah and Khomeini", London: I.B.Tauris.

Childress,Diana (2011), "Equal Rights is our Minimum Demand: The Women's Rights Movement in Iran", Twenty-First Century Books (CT).

Cole, Juan and Keddie, Nikki (ed.) (1986), "Shiism and Social Protest", New Haven: Yale University Press.

Coleman, Isobel (2010), "Paradise Beneath Her Feet: How Women Are Transforming the Middle East", Random House: Council on Foreign Relations Book.

Dabashi, Hamid (2008), "Islamic Liberation Theology: Resisting the Empire", Routledge.

Davis, Nira Yuval and Floya, Anthias (eds.) (1989), "Woman-Nation-State", London: Macmillan.

Ebadi, Shirin (2006), "Iran Awakening: A Memoir of Revolution and Hope", New York: Random House.

Ehteshami, Anoushiravan (1995), "After Khomeinin: The Iranian Second Republic", London: Routledge.

Ellingson, Stephen and Green, M. Christian (eds.) (2002), "Religion and Sexuality in Cross Cultural Perspective", Routledge.

Esfandiari, Haleh (2009), "My Prison, My Home: One Woman's Story of Captivity in Iran", Harper Collin Publishers.

——1997, "Reconstructed Lives: Women and Iran's Islamic Revolution", Washington D.C.: The Woodrow Wilson Centre Press.

Fischer, Michael (1980), "Iran: From Religious Dispute to

Revolution", Cambridge: Harvard University Press.

Friedl, Erika (1991), "The Women of Deh Koh: Lives in an Iranian Village", Penguin Books.

Ganji, Akbar (2008), "The Road to Democracy in Iran", Cambridge: The MIT Press.

Gheissari, Ali (1998), "Iranian Intellectuals in the 20th Century", Austin: University of Texas Press.

—and Vali, Nasr (2006), "Democracy in Iran: History and the Quest for Liberty", Oxford: Oxford University Press.

Göle, Nilüfer (1995), "The Forbidden Modern Civilization and Veiling", Ann Arbor: The University of Michigan Press.

Haeri, Shahla (1987), "Law of Desire: Temporary Marriage in Shi'i Iran", Syracuse, N.Y.: Syracuse University Press.

Hashemi, Nader and Postel, Danny (eds.) (2011), "The People Reloaded: The Green Movement and the Struggle for Iran's Future", Melville House.

Hooglund Eric (ed.) (2002), "Twenty Years of Islamic Revolution: Political and Social Transition in Iran since 1979", Syracuse University Press.

Honarbin-Holliday, Mehri (2009), "Becoming Visible in Iran: Women in Contemporary Iranian Society", Tauris Academic Studies.

Howard, Jane (2002), "Inside Iran: Women's Lives", Washington, DC: Mage Publishers.

Inglehart Ronald and Norris Pippa (2002), "Rising Tide: Gender Equality and Cultural Change around the World", Cambridge: Cambridge University Press.

Joseph, Suad (ed.) (2003), "Encyclopedia of Women and Islamic Cultures", Vol. 1, Leiden and Boston: Brill.

Juchka, Darlene M (ed.) (2001), "Feminism in the Study of Religion: A Reader", Bloomsburry Academic.

Kamrava, Mehran and Dorraj, Manochehr (2008), "Iran Today: An Encyclopaedia of Life in the Islamic Republic", Greenwood Press.

Kandiyoti, Deniz (ed) (1991), "Women, Islam and State", London: Macmillan Press.

Kramer,Martin (1987), "Shi'ism, Resistance and Revolution", Boulder: Westview Press.

Keddie, Nikki (1981), "Roots of Revolution", New Haven and London: Yale University Press.

Kian, Azadeh (2012), "Gendered Citizenship and the Women's Movement in Iran", in Parsi, Rouzbeh (ed.), "Iran: A Revolutionary Republic in Transition".

Kurzman, Charles (2005), "The Unthinkable Revolution in Iran", Cambridge, MA: Harvard University Press.

Lorber, Judith (1994), "Paradoxes of Gender", New Haven, CT: Yale Press.

Maduro, Otto (1982), "Religion and Social Conflicts", Maryknoll, NY: Orbis Books.

Milani, Farzaneh (2013), "Words, Not Swords: Iranian Women Writers and the Freedom of Movement", Syracuse University Press.

Mahmood, Saba (2005), "Politics of Piety: The Islamic Revival and the Feminist Subject", Princeton: Princeton University Press.

Melucci, Alberto (1989), "Nomads of the Present: Social Movements and Individual Needs in Contemporary Society", London: Hutchinson Radius.

Menashri, David (1992), "Education and the making of Modern Iran", Ithaca, NY: Cornell University Press.

Mernissi, Fatima (1987), "Beyond the Veil: Male-Female Dynamics in Modern Muslim Society", second edition, Bloomington: Indiana University Press.

Mir-Hosseini, Ziba (1993), "Marriage on Trial: A Study of Islamic Family Law: Iran and Morocco Compared", London. I.B. Tauris.

—1999, "Islam and Gender: The Religious Debate in Contemporary Iran", Princeton University Press.

—and Tapper, Richard (2006), "Islam and Democracy in Iran: Eshkevari and the Quest for Reform", New York: I.B. Tauris.

Milani, Farzaneh (1992), "Veils and Words: The Emerging Voices of Iranian Women Writers (Contemporary Issues in the Middle East)", Syracuse University Press.

Moallem, Minoo (2005), "Between Warrior Brother and Veiled Sister: Islamic Fundamentalism and Politics of Patriarchy in Iran", Berkeley and Los Angeles: University of California Press.

Moghissi, Haideh (1996), "Populism and Feminism in Iran: Women's Struggle in a Male-Defined Revolutionary Movement", New York: St. Martin's Press.

Moin, Baqer (1999), "Khomeini: Life of the Ayatollah", New York: St. Martin's Press.

Moslem, Mehdi (2002), "Factional Politics in Post Khomeini Iran", Syracuse: University Press.

Nafisi, Azar (2003), "Reading Lolita in Tehran", Random House Publishing Group.

Naghibi, Nima (2007), "Rethinking Global Sisterhood: Western Feminism and Iran", Minneapolis: University of Minnesto Press.

Najmabadi, Afsaneh (1994), "Power, Morality and the New Muslim Womanhood", in Weiner, Myron and Banuazizi, Ali (eds.), 'The Politics of Social Transformation in Afghanistan, Iran and Pakistan', Syracuse University Press.

—2005, "Women with Moustaches and Men without Beards: Gender and Sexual Anxieties of Iranian Modernity", Berkeley: University of California Press.

Nashat, Guity (ed.) (1983), "Women and Revolution in Iran", Boulder: Westview Press.

Nemat,Marina (2008), "Prisoner of Tehran: One Woman's Story of Survival Inside an Iranian Prison", Free Press Books.

Omid, Homa (1994), "Islam and the Post-Revolutionary State in Iran", New York: St. Martin's Press.

Osanloo,Arzoo (2009), "The Politics of Women's Rights in Iran", Princeton, NJ: Princeton University Press.

Paider, Parvin (1995), "Women and the Political Process in Twentieth-Century Iran", Cambridge: Cambridge University Press.

Povey, Tara and Povey, Elaheh Rostami (eds.) (2012), "Women, Power and Politics in 21st Century Iran", Ashgate Publishing Limited.

—Povey, Elaheh Rostami (2010), "Iran's Influence: A Religious-Political State and Society in its Region", London: Zed Books.

Poya, Maryam (1999), "Women, Work and Islamism: Ideology and Resistance in Iran", Zed Books: London.

Qasim, Zaman Muhammmad (2002), "The Ulama in Contemporary Islam: Custodians of Change", Princeton: Princeton University Press.

Ramzan, Nesta (2002), "The Dance of the Rose and the Nightingale (Gender, Culture, and Politics in the Middle East)", Syracuse University Press.

Reeves, Minou (1989), "Female Warriors of Allah: Women and the Islamic Revolution", New York: E.P. Dutton.

Riesebrodt, Martin (1998), "Pious Passion: The Emergence of

Modern Fundamentalism in the United States and Iran", Berkeley, CA: University of California Press.

Ronald, Inglehart and Pippa, Norris (2002), "Rising Tide: Gender Equality and Cultural Change around the World", Cambridge: Cambridge University Press.

Shachar, Ayelet (2001), "Multicultural Jurisdictions: Cultural Differences and Women's Rights", Cambridge: Cambridge University Press.

Samiuddin, Abida and Khanam, R. (2002), "Muslim Feminism and Feminist Movement (Middle-East Asia)", Global Vision Publishing House.

Sansarian, Eliz (1982), "The Women's Rights Movement in Iran", New York: Praeger.

Sedghi, Hamideh (2007), "Women and Politics in Iran: Veiling, Unveiling, and Reveiling", Cambridge University Press.

Schirazi, Asghar (1998), "The Constitution of Iran: Politics and State in the Islamic Republic", John O'Kane (translated), London: I.B. Tauris.

Shahidian, Hammed (2002), "Gender Politics in Islamic Republic", Greenwood Press, London.

——2002, "Emerging Voices in the Women's Movement", Greenwood Press, London.

Shirazi, Faegheh (2001), "The Veil Unveiled: The Hijab in Modern Culture", University Press of Florida.

Smith, Jane I. (1985), "Women, Religion and Social Change in Early Islam", in Yvonne Yazbeck Haddad and Ellison Banks Findly (eds.), 'Women, Religion, and Social Change', Albany: SUNY Press.

Steans, Jill (2006), "Gender and International Relations", Polity Press.

Stowasser, Barbara Freyer (1994), "Women in the Qur'an, Traditions, and Interpretation", New York: Oxford University Press.

Tabari, Azar and Yeganeh, Nahid (eds.) (1982), "In the Shadow of Islam: Women's Movement in Iran", London: Zed Books.

Torab, Azam (2006), "Performing Islam: Gender and Ritual in Iran (Women and Gender: the Middle East and the Islamic World)", Brill Academic Publisher.

Tazmini, Ghoncheh, "Khatami's Iran: The Islamic Republic and the Turbulent Path to Reform", I.B. Tauris.

Vakil, Sanam (2012), "Women and Politics in the Islamic Republic of Iran: Action and Reaction", Bloomsbury Academic.

Wadud, Amina (1999), "Qur'an and Woman: Re-Reading the Sacred Text from a Woman's Perspective", New York: Oxford University Press.

—2006, "Inside the Gender Jihad: Women's Reform in Islam", One World Publications.

Walby, Sylvia (1994), "Theorizing Patriarchy", Cambridge, MA: Blackwell.

—2011, "The Future of Feminism", Polity Press.

Waylen, Georgina (1996), "Analysing Women in Third World Politics", in Haleh Afsar (ed.), 'Women and Politics in Third World', Routledge.

Wiktorowicz, Quintan (2003), "Islamic Activism: A Social Movement Theory Approach", Bloomington: Indiana University Press.

Wright, Robin (2000), "The Last Great Revolution: Turmoil and Transformation in Iran", New York: Alfred A. Knopf.

Yuval-Davis, Nira and Anthias, Floya (eds) (1989), "Woman, Nation and State", London: Macmillan Press.

B.2 Articles

Afkhami, Mahnaz (1997), "Promoting Women's Rights in the Muslim World", *Journal of Democracy,* Vol. 8, No. 1, pp. 157-166.

Afary, Janet (1989), "On the Origins of Feminism in Early 20th Century Iran", *Journal of Womens History,* Vol. 1, No. 2, pp. 65-87.

—2004, "The Human Rights of Middle Eastern and Muslim Women: A Project for the 21st Century", *Human Rights Quarterly,* Vol. 26, No. 1, pp. 106-125.

Afshar, Haleh (2008), "Women and Politics in Iran", *European Journal of Development Research,* Vol. 12, No. 1, June, pp.188-205.

—1985, "Women, State and Ideology in Iran", *Third World Quarterly,* Vol. 7, No. 2, pp. 256-278.

—1982, "Khomeini's Teachings and Their Implications for Women", *Feminist Review,* No. 12, pp. 59-72.

Afzali, Nasrin (2005), "We Do Not Accept Exclusion: A Report on the Campaign against Banning of Iranian Women from

Stardom", available at: http://issuu.com/awid/docs/against-all-odds_iran_eng.

Ahmadi, Fereshteh (2006), "Islamic Feminism in Iran: Feminism in a New Islamic Context", *Journal of Feminist Studies in Religion,* Vol. 22, No. 2, pp. 33-53.

Ahmadi Khorasani, Noushin (2009), "Iranian Women's One Million Signatures Campaign for Equality: The Inside Story", Women's Learning Partnership, available at: http://www.learningpartnership.org/iran-oms-inside-story.

Alamdari, Kazem, "The Power Structure of the Islamic Republic of Iran: Transition from Populism to Clientelism, and Militarization of the Government", *Third World Quarterly,* Vol. 26, No. 8, pp. 1285-1301.

Akbari, Azadeh, "The Women's Movement: An Emerging Power", available at: http://www.lse.ac.uk/IDEAS/publications/reports/pdf/SU002/akbari.pdf.

Alfoneh, Ali (2008), "The Revolutionary Guards Role in Iranian Politics", *Middle East Quarterly,* Vol. 15, No. 4, pp. 3-14.

Amuzegar,Jahangir (2003), "Iran's Crumbling Revolution", *Foreign Affairs,* Vol. 82, No. 1, pp. 44-57.

—2007, "The Ahmadinejad Era: Preparing for the Apocalypse", *Journal of International Affairs,* Vol. 60, No. 2, pp. 35-53.

Ansari, Ali (2008), "Iran under Ahmadinejad: Populism and its Malcontents", *International Affairs,* Vol. 84, No. 4, pp. 683-700.

—2009, "Preliminary Analysis of the Voting Figures in Iran's 2009 Presidential Elections", available at: www.chathamhouse.org/publications/papers/view/10908.

Ashraf, Ahmed (1990), "Theocracy and Charisma: New Men of Power in Iran", *International Journal of Politics, Culture and Society,* Vol. 4, pp. 113-152.

Bahramitash, Roksana (2003), "Islamic Fundamentalism and Women's Economic Role: The Case of Iran", *International Journal of Politics, Culture, and Society,* Vol. 16, No. 4, pp. 551-568.

Bakhtiari, Bahman (1993), "Parliamentary Elections in Iran", *Iranian Studies,* Vol. 26, Nos. 3-4, pp. 375-388.

Banuazizi, Ali (1995), "Faltering Legitimacy: The Ruling Clerics and Civil Society in Contemporary Iran", *International Journal of Politics, Culture, and Society,* Vol. 8, No. 4, pp. 563-578.

Barlow, Rebecca and Akbarzadeh, Shahram (2008), "Prospects for Feminism in the Islamic Republic of Iran", *Human Rights Quarterly,* Vol. 30, No. 1, February, pp. 21-40.

Baavur, Liora Hendelman, "A Mid-Term Assessment of Ahmadinejad's Gender Policy", available at: http://www.aftau.org/site/DocServer/iran_pulse_16.pdf.pdf?docID=2341.

Bayat, Asef (2009), "Iran: Green Wave for Life and Liberty", available at: https://www.opendemocracy.net/article/iran-a-green-wave-for-life-and-liberty.

—2007, "A Women's Non-Movement: What it Means to be a Women's Activist in an Islamic State", *Comparative Studies of South Asia, Africa and the Middle East,* Vol. 27, No. 1, pp. 160-172.

—2005, "Islamism and Social Movement Theory", *Third World Quarterly,* Vol. 26, No. 6, pp. 891-908.

Behrouz, Andra (2003), "Transforming Islamic Family Law: State Responsibility and the Role of Internal Initiative", *Columbia Law Review,* Vol. 103, No. 5, pp. 1136-1162.

Casanova, Jose, "Religion, Politics and Gender Equality in Public Religions Revisited", available at: www.unrisd.org/80256B3C005BCCF9/.../$file/WEBCasvadrftII pdf.

Cincotta, Richard, "Prospects for Ahmadinejad's Call for More Rapid Population Growth in Iran", available at: http://www.stimson.org/summaries/prospects-for-ahmadinejads-call-for-more-rapid-population-growth-in-iran.

Esfandiari, Haleh, "For Women of the Arab Spring: Iranian Women Provide a Warning and a Model", available at: http://www.turkishpolicy.com/dosyalar/files/vol_11no_4%20esfandiari.pdf.

Fathi, Nazila (2005), "Hundreds of Women Protest Sex Discrimination in Iran", available at : http://www.nytimes.com/2005/06/12/international/middleeast/13womencnd.html.

Faruqui, Munis D. (1998), "Iran: Renegotiating a Revolutionary Identity", *Economic and Political Weekly,* Vol. 33, No. 31, pp. 2071-2077.

Ghanea, Nazila (2004), "Human Rights of Religious Minorities and of Women in the Middle East", *Human Rights Quarterly,* Vol. 26, pp.705-729.

Moghissi, Haideh (1991), "Women, Modernization and Revolution in Iran", *Review of Radical Political Economics,* Vol. 23, No. 3-4, pp. 205-223.

Haghayeghi, Mehrdad (1993), "Politics and Ideology in the Islamic Republic of Iran", *Middle Eastern Studies,* Vol. 29, No. 1, pp. 36-52.

Halper, Louise (2005), "Law and Women's Agency in Post-Revolutionary Iran", *Harvard Journal of Law and Gender,* Vol. 28, No. 1, pp. 85-142.

Hanson, Brad (1983), "The Wextoxication of Iran: Depictions and Reaction of Behrangi, Al-e Ahmad and Shariati", *International Journal of Middle East Studies,* Vol. 15, No. 1, pp. 1-23.

Hatem, Mervat (2002), "Gender and Islamism in the 1990s", *Middle East Report,* 222 (Spring), pp. 44-47.

Hoodfar, Homa (1994), "Devices and Desires: Population Policy and Gender Roles in the Islamic Republic", *Middle East Report,* No. 190, pp. 11-17.

—1996, "Bargaining with Fundamentalism: Women and the Politics of Population Control in Iran", *Reproductive Health Matters,* Vol. 4, No. 8, pp. 30-40.

—1999, "The Women's Movement in Iran: Women at the Crossroads of Secularization and Islamicization", available at: http://connection.ebscohost.com/c/articles/2436875/womens-movement-iran-women-crossroads-secularization-islamization.

—and Sadeghi, Fatemeh (2009), "Against All Odds: The Building of a Women's Movement in the Islamic Republic of Iran", available at: http://r4d.dfid.gov.uk/PDF/Outputs/WomenEmpMus/Hoodfar_AgainstAllOdds_Iran.pdf.

—and Sadr, Shadi (2009), "Can Women Act as Agents of a Democratization of Theocracy in Iran"? final research report prepared for the project, 'Religion, Politics and Gender Equality', United Nations Research Institute for Social Development (UNRISD) and Heinrich-Böll-Stiftung, Berlin, Germany and Geneva, Switzerland.

Iran Human Rights Documentation Center (IHRDC), "Silencing the Women's Rights Movement in Iran", available at: http://www.iranhrdc.org/english/publications/reports/3007-

silencing-the-women-s-rights-movement-in-iran.html?p=8.
Joseph, Suad, "Gender and Citizenship in the Arab World", available at: http://iwsaw.lau.edu.lb/publications/al-raida/citizenship-and-gender-in-the.php.
Kadivar,Mohsen (2009), "The Unjust Could Not Be Divine", available at: https://web.stanford.edu/dept/islamic_studies/cgi-bin/web/events/past-events/past-events-for-2008-09.
Kandiyoti, Deniz (1991), "Women, Islam and the State", *Middle East Report,* No. 173, pp. 9-14.
Kian, Azadeh (1995), "Gendered Occupation and Women's Status in Post-Revolutionary Iran", *Middle Eastern Studies,* Vol. 31, No. 3, pp. 407-421.
——1997, "Women and Politics in Post-Islamist Iran: The Gender Conscious Drive to Change", *British Journal of Middle Eastern Studies,*Vol. 24, No. 1, pp. 75-96.
——2010, "Islamic Feminism in Iran: A New Form of Subjugation or the Emergence of Agency"?, Available at: http:/www.sciencespo.fr/ceri/sites/sciencespo.fr.ceri/files/ci_feminism_iran_ak.pdf.
Keddie, Nikki (2007), "Iranian Women's Status and Struggle since 1979", *Journal of International Affairs,* Vol. 60, No. 2, pp. 17-33.
Kurzman, Charles (2001), "Critics Within: Islamic Scholars' Protests against the Islamic State in Iran", *International Journal of Politics, Culture, and Society,* Vol. 15, No. 2, pp. 341-359.
Mahdavi, Shireen (1983), "Women and the Shii Ulama in Iran", *Middle Eastern Studies,* Vol. 19, No. 1, pp. 17-27.
Majbouri, Mehdi, "On the Dynamics of Women's Rights Movement in Iran, 1996-2006", available at: http:/faculty.babson.edu/mmajbouri/documents/papers/womenrights.pdf.
Mahdi, Ali Akbar (2004), "The Iranian Women's Movement: A Century Long Struggle", *Journal of the Muslim World,* Vol. 94, October, pp. 427-448.
——"Iranian Women: Between Islamicization and Globalization", available at: go.owu.edu/~aamahdi/women%20and%20globalization-final.pdf.

Mehrdad, Mashayekhi (2001), "The Revival of the Student Movement in Post-Revolutionary Iran", *International Journal of Politics, Culture, and Society,* Vol. 15, No. 2, pp. 283-313.

Mehran, Golnar (2003), "Paradox of Tradition and Modernity in Female Education in the Islamic Republic of Iran", *Comparative Education Review,* Vol. 47, No. 3, pp. 269-286.

—"Doing and Undoing Gender: Female Higher Education in the Islamic Republic of Iran", available at: http://www.jstor.org/stable/40608077.

—2003, "Khatami, Political Reform and Education in Iran", *Comparative Education,* Vol. 39, No. 3, pp. 311-329.

Mir-Hosseini, Ziba (2002), "The Conservative: Reformist Conflict over Women's Rights in Iran", *International Journal of Politics, Culture, and Society,* Vol. 16, No. 1, pp. 37-53.

Moaddel, Mansoor (1998), "Religion and Women: Islamic Modernism versus Fundamentalism", *Journal for the Scientific Study of Religion,* Vol. 37, No. 1, pp. 108-130.

Moghadam, Valentine M. (1988), "Women, Work and Ideology in the Islamic Republic", *International Journal of Middle East Studies,* Vol. 20, No. 2, pp. 221-243.

—"The Reproduction of Gender Inequality in the Islamic Republic: A Case Study of Iran in the 1980s", *World Development,* No. 19, pp. 1335-1350.

—"Women in the Islamic Republic of Iran: Legal Status, Social Positions, and Collective Action", available at: http://www.wilsoncenter.org/sites/default/files/ValentineMoghadamFinal.pdf.

— "Where Are Iran's Working Women"?, available at: http://www.mei.edu/content/where-are-irans-working-women.

Moghissi, Haideh (1991), "Women, Modernization and Revolution in Iran", *Review of Radical Political Economics,* Vol. 23, No. 3-4, pp. 205-223.

Moinifar, Heshamat Sadat, "Participation of Women in Iran's Polity", available at: http://www.law.tohoku.ac.jp/gcoe/wp-content/uploads/2011/03/gemc_04_cate2_4.pdf.

Mojab, Shahrzad (2001), "Theorizing the Politics of Islamic Feminism", *Feminist Review,* No. 69, pp. 124-146.

Najmabadi, Afsaneh (2004), "The Morning After: Travail of Sexuality and Love in Modern Iran", *International Journal of*

Middle East Studies, Vol. 36, No. 3, pp. 367-385.

Povey, Elaheh (2001), "Feminist Contestation of Institutional Domain in Iran", *Feminist Review,* No. 69, pp. 44-72.

—"Women and Work in Iran (Part 1)", available at: http://www.stateofnature.org/?p=5243.

Rafizadeh, Majid (2014), "The Islamic State of Iran and Gender Discrimination", available at: http://www.frontpagemag.com/2014/majid-rafizadeh/the-islamic-state-of-iran-and-gender-discrimination.

Ramazani, Nesta (1993), "Women in Iran: the Revolutionary Ebb and Flow", *Middle East Journal,* Vol. 47, No. 3, pp. 409-428.

Razavi, Shahra (2006), "Islamic Politics, Human Rights and Women's Claims for Equality in Iran", *Third World Quaterly,* Vol. 27, No. 7, pp. 1223-1238.

Rezai-Rashti, Goli M., "The Future of Iran: Educational Reform Women and Education in the Islamic Republic of Iran: Repressive Policies, Unexpected Outcomes", available at: http://www.li.com/docs/default-source/default-document-library/women-and-education-in-the-islamic-republic-of-iran-repressive-policies-unexpected-outcomes.

Robin, Wright, "Iran's New Revolution", *Foreign Affairs,* Vol. 79, No. 1, pp. 133-145.

—1997, "Iran's Greatest Political Challenge: Abdol Karim Soroush", *World Policy Journal,* Vol. 14, No. 2, pp. 67-74.

Shachar, Ayelet, "Religion, State, and the Problem of Gender: New Modes of Citizenship and Governance in Diverse Societies', available at: lawjournal.mcgill.ca/userfiles/other/410530-1225240850_Shachar.pdf.

Sadeghi, Fatemeh (2009), "Foot Soldiers of the Islamic Republic's Culture of Modesty", *Middle East Report,* No. 250, The Islamic Revolution at 30, Spring, pp. 50-55.

—2007, "Women and the Islamic Revolution: A Story of a Muslim Woman", available at: http://issuu.com/awid/docs/sp-case-study-iran.

Sadri, Ahmad (2001), "The Varieties of Religious Reform: Public Intelligentsia in Iran", *International Journal of Politics, Culture, and Society,* Vol. 15, No. 2, pp. 271-282.

Shahrokni, Nazanin (2009), "All the President's Women", *Middle East Report,* No. 253,Winter, pp. 2-6.

Shavarini, Mitra (2005), "The Feminisation of Iranian Higher Education", *International Review of Education,* Vol. 51, No. 4, pp. 329-347.

Tabari, Azar (1986), "The Women's Movement in Iran: A Hopeful Prognosis", *Feminist Studies,* Vol. 12, No. 2, pp. 342-360.

Talattof, Kamran (1997), "Iranian Women's Literature: From Pre-evolutionary Social Discourse to Post-revolutionary Feminism", *International Journal of Middle East Studies,* Vol. 29, No. 4, pp. 531-559.

Tamadonfar, Mehran (2001), "Islam, Law, and Political Control in Contemporary Iran", *Journal for the Scientific Study of Religion,* Vol. 40, No. 2, pp. 205-219.

Takeyh, Ray (2003), "Iran at a Crossroads", *Middle East Journal,* Vol. 57, No. 1, pp. 42-56.

Tremayne, Soraya (2006), "Modernity and Early Marriage in Iran: A View from Within", *Journal of Middle East Women's Studies,* Vol. 2, No. 1, pp. 65-94.

Vafai, Gholam, "Iran: New Women's Inheritance Law is Enforced", available at: http://www.loc.gov/lawweb/servlet/lloc_news?disp3_l205401290_text.

Vahdat, Farzin (2003), "Post-Revolutionary Islamic Discourses on Modernity in Iran: Expansion and Contraction of Human Subjectivity", *International Journal of Middle East Studies,* Vol. 35, No. 4, pp. 599-631.

Wadud, Amina, "Woman Leads US Muslims to Prayer", available at: http://news.bbc.co.uk/2/hi/americas/4361931.stm.

Yeganeh, Nahid (1993), "Nationalism and Islam in Contemporary Political Discourse in Iran", *Feminist Review,* No. 44, pp. 3-18.

B.3 Newspapers

Payvand Iran News
Women's UN Report Network
Fars News Agency
Islamic Republic News Agency
Iran News Daily
Iran Daily
Iran Press News

Index

Index